# GASKIN

*For Lynn with love*

# GASKIN

## — PAUL BEDFORD —

HISTORY INTO PRINT

First published by
History into Print, 56 Alcester Road,
Studley, Warwickshire B80 7LG in 2006
www.history-into-print.com

ISBN 1 85858 312 8

A Cataloguing in Publication Record
for this title is available from the British Library.

Typeset in Baskerville
Printed in Great Britain by
Cromwell Press Ltd.

# CONTENTS

## *About The Author*

# PAUL BEDFORD

Paul is a teacher who works in a school in Staffordshire. When not in the classroom, Paul follows the results of Walsall Football Club and Warwickshire County Cricket Club. He also enjoys attempting to keep fit and walking, although the benefit of this may be offset by a love of cooking, good food and wine. Paul is married to Lynn, also a teacher, and lives in Staffordshire with his two step – sons, Andrew and Thomas.

# INTRODUCTION

My grandfather, John Emery was born in January 1892, some six months after Henry Thomas Gaskin had come into the world. Both men were coal miners and family tradition has it that the two men knew each other, albeit briefly. This is why the Gaskin case has always held a fascination for me.

This book is the culmination of around ten years of research and writing, much of it at weekends and holidays. During this time, I have received help and encouragement from a number of people and sources. I will attempt to give them credit and apologise in advance if I have omitted anyone.

Firstly, the staff at Cannock Library, in the Local History section, whose knowledge and help was unfailing. Mention should also be given to the staff at both Lichfield Record Office and the County Record office at Stafford. Many questions were asked and once more the patience and professionalism displayed never flagged.

My research took me further afield, and the assistance received from Birmingham City Archives was exceptionally welcome. In particular, access was given to MS 1815/11 HM Prison Winson Green which gave essential information on Gaskin's execution.

Considerable help was also shown by the staff at the British Newspaper Library in London, who helped me track down a reference to Gaskin in the News of the World from 1919.

Friendly assistance was a feature of the National Archive in London which enabled me to discover previously unknown information about Gaskin's brief flirtation with the army on 1910.

Closer to home I would like to thank Dr. David Blanchard for taking time away from his administering to the sick to offer his considerable knowledge in making Dr. Butter's Post Mortem report on Elizabeth Gaskin understandable to a layman.

My thanks also go to Mrs. Jenny Lawrence for her help and advice when proof reading my manuscript. It is without doubt that the quality would have been much poorer without her input.

The superb cover is down to Ian Pritchard and his artistic and technical expertise. I hope the text matches it.

I would like to place on record the help and support from many members of my family, in particular to my wife Lynn, without whose encouragement this book would never have been completed. I owe her an enormous debt.

*Paul Bedford*

*Chapter One*

# EXECUTION

Few people if any noticed the balding moustachioed figure arrive at Winson Green Prison Birmingham on Thursday 7th August 1919. He would have preferred it so; for John Ellis disliked calling attention to himself. For nineteen years he had supplemented his income from his barbers' shop in Rochdale by acting as a public executioner.

Ellis was a punctilious man. He prided himself on the thoroughness of his preparations at the many executions he had attended, firstly as an assistant and then as the principal executioner. Winson Green provided challenges to Ellis. The execution chamber was just a few yards from the condemned cell; indeed, a pair of yellow doors opened from the cell into the chamber itself. Ellis knew he would have to change some of his normal routines. He was a humane man and took immense pride that his techniques, honed over the years, had led to improvements in executions, making them quicker and less barbaric. Therefore, Gaskin would have to be taken from the condemned cell while Ellis checked the rope, beam and trap doors. Ellis was aware of the deep booming sound that these doors made when the lever was pulled. He did not want this sound to unnerve his next client. This Ellis was certain would lead to problems on the following morning. So whilst Gaskin, accompanied by two warders, was walking around the prison yard, Ellis worked feverishly. He knew from the prison record that his victim was 5 feet 7 ½ inches tall and weighed 13 stones and 5 pounds. A bag filled with sand to this exact weight was attached to the rope by Ellis and his assistant for this execution, William Willis.

Next, Ellis checked the rope carefully making sure there were no cracks in the lining. The lever was then pulled. A loud boom reverberated through the corridor and cells in that part of the prison. It was essential that this was kept from Gaskin. The bag would be left dangling from the rope overnight to take out any stretch left in the fibres. Ellis then left the execution cell to the care of the prison warders. As normal, in these circumstances, the cell was locked for the night.

Once Gaskin had been returned to his cell, Ellis took the opportunity to observe his client. He may have already caught a glimpse of him in the exercise yard, but Ellis usually tried to have a second and closer inspection of the condemned man. Silently he raised the cover of the inspection hole of Gaskin's cell door. He knew that Gaskin was a powerful miner, but in this instance Ellis would have focused his professional eye on one part of the prisoner's anatomy; his neck.

Ellis wanted to ensure that he gave Gaskin the correct drop. It had to be of sufficient length to dislocate the neck immediately thus ensuring that Gaskin did not suffer pain. What met Ellis's gaze was a thick and muscular neck. Ellis would have now made a decision about the length of drop. According to the guidance issued by the Home Office a man of Gaskin's stature should have received a drop of 5 feet 4 inches. Ellis, as a matter of expertise and experience, usually added several inches to this advice.

He realised that a neck such as Gaskin's may not be properly dislocated with such a short drop. Gaskin was a man in fine physical condition. His army service in a Royal Engineer's Tunnelling Company together with his employment in a mine had meant that Gaskin was as described at his trial as "a man of fine physique". Ellis's next task was to consult with the prison Medical Officer W. Cassels. It was rare for the Medical Officer to overrule the expertise of the executioner. It did not happen on this occasion. Ellis convinced Cassels that a drop of 6 feet 3 inches was needed. Cassels would not have wanted to risk the awkward questions that would have followed if Gaskin's neck had not been dislocated immediately. He thus concurred with Ellis's advice.

Ellis and Willis were shown to their quarters for the night. This was a cell nearby that they would share for the night. A meal and a cup of tea would have been taken inside. However, Ellis would not have remained in the cell all night. He had visited Winson Green on a number of occasions and had forged friendships with a number of the warders. Ellis had a traditional way of passing the evening. He and some of the warders would have set up a card school. Often these sessions would last late into the night. It passed the time and took Ellis's mind off the somewhat grisly task that faced him on the following morning. Ellis rarely slept well on the night before an execution.

If Ellis was having problems with insomnia, these must have been minimal compared to those of Gaskin. He had known since the failure of his appeal on the 21st July that his execution was fixed for Friday 8th August. He now faced his last night on earth. Gaskin was kept company by a team of warders experienced in watching over condemned prisoners. They were sympathetic to the pressures faced by the prisoner. They were adept at fielding the questions and worries of a man facing imminent death. Those doors simply led to a little used store room.

It is doubtful if Henry Thomas Gaskin enjoyed a good night's sleep on that night. Various thoughts must have flitted across his mind. If only I hadn't played truant from school; if only I hadn't tried to derail a train; if only I hadn't stolen that silver watch; if only I hadn't demanded money with menaces; if only I hadn't burgled those shops in Cannock; if only I had never met Elizabeth Talbot and married her in 1913. A man whose life had been somewhat tortured by doubt and misfortune now had to face up to the final night of mental anguish. The night would have undoubtedly been the longest that Gaskin had faced.

At six thirty on the morning of Friday 8th August 1919, John Ellis and his assistant, William Willis, were awoken by one of the warders bearing both of them a welcome cup of tea. Ellis was now keen to get on with the task in hand. He and Willis made their way to the execution shed, having first ensured that all was well with Gaskin. A quick check through the peep hole was enough to ascertain that all was as well as it could be in the condemned cell. Ellis and Willis firstly removed the sack filled with sand from the noose. The rope was then checked for a final time before being carefully measured and coiled at the precise mark for the correct drop. Ellis and Willis then confirmed the arrangements with the Sheriff of Staffordshire, F. A. Bolton and the Governor of Winson Green prison, E. Goldie-Taubman. Ellis knew from vast experience that a minimum of time was required in order that the prisoner was not unduly made to suffer. Ellis then verified that only a minute was necessary before eight o' clock for both him and his assistant to make sure Gaskin was ready. Ellis and Willis then departed to eat some breakfast.

In the condemned cell, Gaskin was consuming his last meal. Whether the cliché of the prisoner eating a hearty breakfast applied to Gaskin we do not know. Certainly the meal eaten by most condemned men was anything but hearty, usually consisting of some bread, perhaps an egg and a cup of tea. The warders then did their best to ready Gaskin for his ordeal. At around seven forty-five the Reverend J. W. Blakemore was shown into the cell. If this person filled Gaskin with a feeling of doom then it would almost certainly have given Ellis a moment of discomfort. Blakemore had been the Chaplain at Chelmsford prison for the execution of Samuel Dougal on 14th July 1903. Blakemore had been unable to obtain a confession of guilt from Dougal and had determined to have one last attempt. Unfortunately this took place just as Billy Billingham, assisted by Ellis, was about to pull the lever. To say this was unusual was to say the least. It was unheard of. Momentary panic set in. However Blakemore obtained his confession and the execution went ahead a few seconds later. Billingham was very upset at this incident as he saw his duty was to execute the prisoner with a minimum of agonising delay. Now, sixteen years later, that thought would have flashed across Ellis's mind. Blakemore had been transferred to Birmingham a short time after the death of Dougal. His and Ellis's paths had crossed again in 1916 for the execution of William Allan Butler. Now they were passing again.

Blakemore would have sought to gain a final confession from Gaskin. It is doubtful if he experienced any difficulty. There was no question that Gaskin was guilty and he had expressed remorse at his trial. Blakemore would have been confident when he made his way to the scaffold that he would have no reason to interrupt. Blakemore then began saying the prayers he was obliged by law to incant. Whilst he was doing this Gaskin would probably have been saying his goodbyes to the warders who had looked after him since his incarceration at Winson Green. At one minute to eight the cell door opened. The Governor, the Sheriff of Staffordshire and the Medical Officer would have filed into the cell. The yellow doors leading to the execution cell were opened. The officials started to file into the small execution room. Space was at a premium; the execution cell was only some fourteen feet square and painted white to cover the bare bricks. William Willis went to stand behind Gaskin and pulled the powerful miner's hands behind his back where he pinioned them with the thick leather strap. Whilst this was going on Ellis would have stood in front of Gaskin. "When you get to the trapdoor, stand on the chalk mark and then look me in the eyes. It will soon be over for you if you do as I ask". Ellis walked in front of his victim as was his custom. He reckoned that this saved time and thus reduced the suffering of the prisoner. Gaskin was probably bemused by the proceedings especially as he had no doubt been given a large tot of brandy on the advice of Ellis by one of the warders. The grim party walked the few steps from the condemned cell to the execution shed.

When Gaskin arrived on the scaffold, having walked with firm confident steps, events moved with frightening speed. He stood as instructed on the chalked cross. Ellis produced a white cotton hood which he placed over Gaskin's head. Meanwhile Willis would have been kneeling behind the prisoner strapping Gaskin's legs together. Ellis placed the noose around Gaskin's neck, over the hood and then stepped off the trapdoors, pulling the lever. The doors fell away with a boom. Gaskin would not have heard them. His fall into blackness lasted one third of a second before the jerk of the noose dislocated his neck. Now he was deeply unconscious as his life ebbed away.

Outside a crowd of around two hundred people had gathered. Just after eight the prison bell began to toll. A prison warder appeared to pin up two notices on the front gate. One was a declaration, signed by Goldie-Taubman, Bolton and Blakemore. It read quite simply, if formally, "Judgement of death was this day executed on Henry Thomas Gaskin". A second notice was signed by Dr. Cassels to state that he had examined the body "on whom judgement of death was this day executed in the said form and that on examination I found that the said Henry Thomas Gaskin was dead".

This was a moot point. Gaskin at this juncture was probably not dead, or at least not clinically dead. The bruising on his neck reported on the register of executed criminals would indicate that death arrived sometime after the initial jolt which dislocated the vertebrae. Indeed executed prisoners were left hanging in the execution pit for a full hour after the execution, presumably to ensure that strangulation was complete. Gaskin would of course have been in no pain. To all intent and purpose he was as good as dead. The precise time of his death, however, will never be known.

After the hour was up Gaskin's lifeless form was gently pulled up out of the pit by the men given the task of burying his body. The order for burial had been signed by the Coroner of the City of Birmingham, Isaac S. Bradley. His body was stripped of the clothing he had been wearing for the execution and was then placed, naked, in a shell made of cheap wood. Holes would then have been cut in the lid of the shell before it was placed over the body. The shell was then carried to the south east corner of the stone yard within the precincts of Winson Green Prison. A grave had been re-opened and the makeshift coffin placed by the side of the grave. The lid was then lifted and quick lime sprinkled liberally over Gaskin's body. The lid was then put back in place and the coffin shell filled with water. Gaskin's remains were then lowered into the grave and the coffin covered up. A note was made as to its precise position, adjacent to the asylum grounds, roughly fifty yards from the Bailiff's Quarters and some fourteen feet from the new workshops.

Henry Thomas Gaskin had been laid to rest. Yet there was no indication that his mortal remains were so positioned. The Home office and perhaps the Prison authorities were worried about murderers becoming the objects of hero worshippers who might be tempted to exhume bodies for such a purpose. There may also have been concern that family members might also pester the prison for visiting rights to the site, although this would surely have been unlikely. Nonetheless, the practice of marking the wall with a named plaque was suspended. Gaskin was placed in and presumably remains in an unmarked grave.

## Chapter Two

# EARLY YEARS

On October 4th, 1890, in the parish church of the small agricultural village of Shenstone, a marriage took place. A marriage that was like any other that had taken place in the village. Henry Joseph Albert Gaskin, a 27 year old stonemason, and native of the village, took as his lawful married wife Harriett Eliza Poole, an 18 year old spinster and also a native of the same village. Shenstone had always been a farming community. Both the father of the groom and the father of the bride were agricultural labourers, men used to hard work and fresh air. William Gaskin was no doubt proud of his son. After all Henry had served a long apprenticeship in order to become a stonemason and this would mean he was a skilled craftsman able to provide a living above that offered by a mere labourer for his new wife. William left the signing of the register to Thomas Poole, the father of the bride and to her older sister, Elizabeth, perhaps suggesting that reading and writing was not in the repertoire of the Gaskin family.

The wedding was also a proud moment for the Poole family. Thomas had married Agnes Elizabeth Proffitt on October 15th 1850. Their family had been late starting. In 1866, Elizabeth had arrived, followed in January 1870 by Catherine and finally in March 1872, the family was completed with the birth of Harriett. No doubt the Pooles also considered Henry Gaskin to be a good catch for their youngest daughter. He was considerably older than she was and was a known quantity, being sober, God fearing and hard working. It augured well for the future.

Yet, within a few short months changes had taken place in the lives of the young couple. Henry's career as a stonemason came to a sudden end. Whether this was a conscious decision or whether forced upon him by circumstance is not clear. What is certain is that within twelve months Henry was a sawyer, working at a wood mill. This must have been seen as rather a come down and perhaps began to chip away at the self confidence of Henry and of the trust placed in him by Harriet and indeed both families. The young couple had also moved away from Shenstone to the nearby city of Lichfield where they found a dwelling on Stowe Street.

The disappointment of Henry's change of circumstance was no doubt offset by the news, early in 1891, that Harriet was pregnant. The young couple and their respective families were delighted with this news. However, the pregnancy was not an easy one. Harriet had a difficult time, suffering from melancholia for sixteen weeks and remaining in a low state throughout her confinement. Perhaps this was due to the sudden realisation that events were not quite turning out as she first thought. She was, after all, a young woman of nineteen and her life appeared to have taken a turn for the worse. The pregnancy, which to some would have been the natural culmination of her marriage to Henry, had almost become a millstone around the young woman's neck.

Nonetheless, the pregnancy went its full term and both Henry and Harriet were pleased, if not delighted, to announce to their families on 22nd July 1891 the birth of, to all intent and purpose, a healthy baby son. No doubt after such a difficult pregnancy the celebrations may have been tempered with relief. The birth was registered by Harriet on 26th August. Interestingly the child was named Thomas Henry Gaskin.

There was genuine pleasure and joy in the Gaskin household. On the 6th September 1891, at St. Chad's in Lichfield the christening ceremony took place. The new addition to the family now gloried in the name of Henry Thomas Gaskin, both forenames being a mark of respect to the father of the child and to the father of the mother. The ceremony was performed by the vicar of St. Chad's, the Reverend J. C. Tattersall. No doubt a splendid time was had by all who attended this happy family occasion.

Two years later, the Gaskin family were anticipating another happy event. Harriett was again pregnant and it would appear that the problems experienced during her first pregnancy did not materialise this time. Towards the end of 1893 a second child was born, a sister for Henry. By this time there had been another change in circumstances. The Gaskins had moved back to Shenstone, perhaps to be closer to both halves of the family. Henry senior had yet again changed his job. He was now a waggoner. Not as skilled a job as his previous employment, but he now had a growing family to provide for. The parish church of St. John the Baptist at Shenstone was the venue for the second Gaskin christening. On the 28th January 1894, the first daughter of the Gaskin family was named Agnes Mary Gaskin. The child's name again was chosen in honour of a member of the family, this time Harriett's mother. The service was conducted by William Quibell, the Curate of Shenstone.

One thing is clear. The young Henry did not enjoy good health. He was always being referred to the doctor whilst growing up and this would have had an impact upon his schooling. There is evidence of frequent absence because of severe headaches. Doctor Taylor told his mother, Harriett, that Henry would need a lot of tender care and that he would need careful looking after. There is also evidence that Henry suffered from mental problems. His own mother stated that he had been strange all his life. Indeed an incident that took place when Henry was around seven years of age would confirm this. The young Henry was sent to wash his hands properly. This was hardly an unusual request. Yet to Henry it was far more than he was prepared to do. Instead, Henry got a scarf and tied it tightly around his neck falling in a semi-conscious state on the floor. This must have been very shocking and frightening for his mother and indeed for the rest of the family. Clearly the eldest of the Gaskin's children was anything but stable mentally. As a result of Henry's problems he came to depend on his mother, more so perhaps than upon his father. After all, his mother was always there for him. The headaches were fairly frequent and it would appear somewhat severe. They were also hereditary. Both Mrs. Gaskin and her father suffered from similar problems. Thomas Poole had tried to commit suicide by cutting his own throat although he recovered from the attempt and went on to live to the ripe old age of 80, dying in Lichfield infirmary. Around the turn of the twentieth century the Gaskin family made an important decision. Perhaps it was motivated by the lure of greater financial rewards, or perhaps to provide a fresh start for the children. It may well have been the fact that Harriett found herself pregnant for a third time. The upshot was a change of career for Henry senior and a change of location for the family. The 1901 census records that Henry Gaskin was now employed as a colliery fireman at the newly opened Littleton Colliery. He and his family were now living at 48, Stafford Road, Huntington, in rented accommodation. Henry junior was now in his tenth year and his sister, Agnes, was now seven years of age. A third child had been born in February 1901 and had been baptised at St Luke's parish church in Cannock on the 3rd March 1901. The new addition to the family was another sister for Henry and Agnes. Her name was given as Mary Louisa Gaskin. Any celebrations at this wonderful news were short lived. The baby did not live long, dying on the 6th July 1901, of convulsions, after only five and a half months. Her mother was present at the death and registered the event on 8th July.

*Chapter Three*

# MEET THE TALBOTS

There was little that was remarkable about the Talbot family of Brindley Heath. On 10th June 1889, at St Peter's church, Hednesford, Henry Charles Talbot, a 19 year old bachelor and a miner by occupation, married Emily Ann Bailey a spinster of the parish aged 22. The groom had been born in Brocton, near Stafford and his new wife had been born in Brewood, Staffordshire, suggesting that in both cases their family stock was rooted in agriculture. The arrival of deep mined coal in Hednesford in the period from 1850 meant rapid growth in what had been a series of agricultural hamlets. By the turn of the century Hednesford was a thriving industrial town with an influx of workers for the numerous mines and, of course, the various trades associated with a rapidly growing community.

Interestingly, the bride does not give any details about her own father on the marriage certificate. The groom's father was William Talbot, a labourer. The marriage was witnessed by Joseph Talbot, the groom's brother and by Maria Arkley a friend of the bride. The ceremony was performed by George Whitehouse, a curate at St Peter's.

It may well be that the marriage was considered to be a necessity. Perhaps the permission of the bride's father had not been forthcoming. There is a suggestion that Emily was pregnant. The young couple both gave their address as Hednesford on the certificate of marriage, indicating that they were already living together.

This suggestion is given further credence by the fact that the first born child of the couple, Abner William Talbot, was born in

1889. The first born son was not baptised either at St. Peter's or at the parish church of St. Luke at Cannock, an unusual step at that time when observance of religious custom was far more prevalent than it is now.

Henry Talbot was a stallman by trade. In simple terms, he mined coal at the face in the colliery. This was a relatively well paid job, but it was also very dangerous. Accidents in collieries at that time were commonplace. The safety record of the collieries in the Cannock Chase coalfield was no worse than pits elsewhere. This should not detract from the almost daily risk of death or serious injury. However, it would seem that Henry Talbot was fortunate; there is no record of any injury whilst working down the pit.

Life therefore, seemed to be progressing smoothly for the Talbot family. A daughter, Mary Ann Talbot, was born in 1892. A third child, another girl was born on 15th August 1894. She was baptised on 5th September of that year at St. Peter's. Her name was Elizabeth Talbot. Within two years there was another addition to the Talbot household with the birth of a second son. Once more the venue for the baptism was St. Peter's. The name chosen was unusual even for that time. The fourth child of Henry and Emily Talbot being named Uriah. The ceremony was performed by Byrom Holland on November 29th 1896. Still the family was not complete, for in 1899 a fifth child was born; a third daughter, named Kate Talbot. Then, perhaps as somewhat of a surprise a sixth child was born into the Talbot household. This birth took place on the 10th October, 1909. The child was the third son of the Talbot family rounding off things nicely. The name given to this boy was Fred Talbot, the baptism taking place again at St. Peter's on the 3rd January 1910.

This steady but regular enlargement of the Talbot household necessitated a move for the family. On the 1901 census the address for the Talbots is given as 99, Bradbury Lane, Hednesford. By the time young Fred had arrived on the scene, the family had moved to 72, Brindley Heath. Presumably a slightly larger house was needed to accommodate a by now, larger family. The gap between the birth of the fifth and sixth children is worthy of comment, but was by no means unusual. There may, however, have been more comment made at the time by neighbours.

Education, it would appear was not high on the list of Talbot priorities for on the 6th October, 1902 at Cannock, Henry Talbot was fined six shillings with an additional four shillings and sixpence costs for failing to send his children to school on a regular basis. This was followed on the 3rd November by an Attendance Order insisting that the Talbot boys attend West Hill Boys' School, thus incurring a further five shillings in costs. This was money that the Talbot family could ill afford.

If this was not bad enough, by 1904, the Talbots had hit rock bottom. At Penkridge on the 15th August they were both charged and found guilty of neglecting their children. The family was in rags, dirty and verminous, with the children dependent upon their neighbours for food. It also became apparent that Emily Talbot had a drinking habit.

The upshot of the case was a fine of five shillings together with costs of eight shillings. Clearly neither Henry nor Emily was inclined to pay and as a result, Henry was sent to gaol for ten days hard labour with Emily receiving seven days. The children would presumably have been looked after by the same caring neighbours, or possibly sent to the workhouse.

This was followed on the 17th December 1904 with a further prosecution for Emily Talbot. She was found guilty of being drunk and disorderly in Station Road. Not the most serious of crimes, but nevertheless incurring a fine of two shillings and sixpence with five shillings in costs being added to it. This was more financial strain on inadequate resources for the Talbot family to bear.

1906 brought yet more misery and despair for the Talbots. On the 14th May the eldest son, Abner, now seventeen, was found guilty, along with James Hawkins, aged fifteen, of stealing four pigeons. Whether these were for food or for racing is no longer clear. What was more certain was the fine of fourteen shillings imposed on each young man by the court at Cannock. Once again the Talbot family was faced with a self inflicted attack on slender finances.

Unfortunately, 1906 had not yet finished with the Talbots. On the 6th December, Mary Ann Talbot accused George Nutting of being the father of her child that had been born in the workhouse at Green Heath on the 9th January. This, it must be remembered, would have been a social stigma of note. Children born outside marriage were not unheard of but were relatively uncommon. What made this shocking was the age of the mother. She was only fourteen, hardly more than a child herself. The case was not proved sufficiently for the court to find in her favour and the order was not served by the authorities.

However, in 1907 an incident occurred that would have disturbed the equilibrium of the Talbot household. On 12th January Henry Talbot received a warrant for ejection from their house. This would have been somewhat of a body blow for the family, especially after the difficult problems they had faced in the previous year. The warrant had a time limit of twenty one days and clearly this was enough time for the Talbots to find the money they owed. The prospect of being thrown out on the street would have seemed very real.

Soon the family were again reeling. Their eldest son, Abner, was prosecuted for theft. The 18 year old was summonsed in connection with the taking of partridge eggs on 6th June. Edgar Wells, a game keeper to Mr. J. P. Gardner, stated that he saw Abner Talbot in the distance coming from the direction of a partridge nest which Wells had seen previously and which he knew contained 13 eggs. He lost sight of Talbot but later, with P. C. Bradley, went to 72, Brindley Heath where Abner Talbot admitted that he had six of the eggs, and three smaller boys had two eggs each. Talbot was fined fifteen shillings and sixpence including costs. This was a considerable sum of money for a mining family to find in 1907. The prospect of finding the money was beyond the family and as a result Abner was sent to prison to face ten days of hard labour.

Clearly though, Abner had still not learned his lesson. For within a matter of four months he was back before the magistrates. In conjunction with John Gannon from Hill Top and Robert Smith, from Brindley Heath, Abner was charged with stealing a bicycle on 13th October, 1907, the property of William Frazer of Anglesey Street, Hednesford. Gannon and Smith were also charged with the theft of a bicycle lamp, tool bag and spanner, belonging to Fred Brown of Bishton Hall.

Frazer described to the court his journey from Hednesford to Rugeley, where he placed his bicycle outside the Black Horse Hotel in that town. It was, he recalled, safe at 7:00pm, yet only forty five minutes later it had disappeared. Together with P. C. Bradley and P. C. Beech, Frazer went to the home of Gannon where he identified his machine, now in parts.

Mary Gannon said that her brother came home on the 10th October with a bicycle and that he and Smith took it to pieces. Gannon said that Talbot had stolen the bicycle and that he and Smith had taken it from him on the Rugeley Road. The two of them had then hidden the machine behind a hedge and then fetched it the next day. Abner Talbot claimed that he had been persuaded to steal the bicycle by Gannon and Smith.

It also transpired that Talbot had stolen the equipment belonging to Fred Brown, something that would have hardly added to the credibility of his defence. Indeed, Gannon and Smith were both fined £1 and 13 shillings costs. Abner Talbot was given three weeks in prison although this was reduced to fourteen days on representation from his solicitor. Yet he now faced his second incarceration in less than a year.

In 1908 the Talbot family had still not finished with the courts. On 2nd October Mary Ann charged John Thomas Spooner with deserting her child. Whether this was a second baby is not clear.

Certainly the case was far from certain and as a result the magistrates decided not to arrest the young man concerned and charged Mary Ann two shillings costs.

Just after the birth of Fred, however, a further problem reared its head. It may well be that one of the causes of the problem was that very birth. A new baby would have placed a strain on a delicately balanced financial situation. Perhaps the response of Elizabeth and Uriah was to try and help the family.

On the 28th March 1910, Elizabeth and her brother stole a pair of boots from inside the doorway of Charles Owen, a bootmaker, in Hednesford. Elizabeth's age was given as 15 and that of her brother Uriah was given as 11. After stealing the boots the two Talbot children then made their way to Cannock where they tried to offer them to William T. Lanspeary, the pawnbroker. Lanspeary, showing commendable wit, asked who owned the boots. Elizabeth claimed that the boots belonged to her mother. Clearly suspicious as the boots were brand new, Lanspeary asked Elizabeth to return to his shop with her mother. The Talbot children fled the shop. Needless to say Elizabeth did not return with her mother. Nor for that matter did Uriah. However, the local police did pay the Talbot household a visit. Elizabeth admitted stealing the boots and trying to pawn them. The boots in question had by this time been returned to Mr. Owen. At a specially convened children's court both Elizabeth and Uriah were bound over to be of good behaviour under the terms of the Probation of Offenders Act.

The first decade of the new century had been a challenging one for the Talbot family of Brindley Heath. Both Henry and Emily Talbot had tasted imprisonment. Their eldest daughter had found herself pregnant at least once and at the tender age of fourteen. Abner, the eldest, had been before the courts on three occasions and had served two terms in gaol. Elizabeth and Uriah had been bound over and subjected to supervision orders by a juvenile court. It appeared that life could only get better in the second decade.

## Chapter Four

# HENRY GASKIN'S SCHOOL DAYS

It is often said that school days are the best days of a person's life. Whether this is true or not depends in all probability on the experiences of that person. In the case of Henry Thomas Gaskin it is doubtful that he would have made such a claim. It would seem that Gaskin did not really enjoy the opportunities offered to him at Walhouse National School, on the Penkridge Road in Cannock. Following the family's move from Shenstone to Huntington this endowed school was the one chosen by Mr. and Mrs. Gaskin for their eldest and only son.

The school enjoyed an excellent local reputation. In the frequent visits by the School Inspectors, the school scored well in terms of the teaching that it provided for its students. The staffing of the school was led by Mr. H. Walker the headmaster, and at the time of Gaskin, included Mr. Mears, Mr. Poyner, Mr. Tennant who had joined the school from Chadsmoor and Miss Baker. All of these teachers were amongst the best available in the Cannock area at that period. The school, due to its endowment from the Church of England, also had the assistance of the Reverend Baylis and the Reverend G. L. Davey.

There were some variances between subjects. Reading and spelling scored particularly well in the Inspectors' eyes, as did history, arithmetic and singing by rote. Geography and current affairs were less spectacular and at the time of Gaskin rated as poor. The school also had Diocesan inspections which assessed the quality of the religious teaching offered by the school. These were split into three divisions with 42 pupils reaching the highest standard, 41 achieving the second standard and 55 attaining the third standard. It is not recorded which level of achievement Gaskin was able to secure.

There would appear to have been the usual problems associated with a boys' school of around 130 pupils of ages ranging from around five to thirteen. One difficulty was the accommodation which the school could offer. As a popular establishment, Walhouse struggled to meet the demand that it faced on a daily basis. It was over subscribed and there were frequent references to pupils having to be turned away.

Other factors also affected attendance at the school. Rain and snow were all that some pupils needed to see in order to find an excuse not to go to school, although in many such cases lack of adequate clothing may have influenced the decisions made by local mothers. Mud and a very uneven playground were amongst the other problems that staff and pupils had to contend with. The school also had cess pits rather than mains sewerage and the Inspectors made much of the inadequate number of urinals for over one hundred boys, there being only five. A further and more serious problem was that of running water down the walls of the classrooms.

The boys were not angels. This is not to say that discipline was a problem. Indeed, the basic standard offered by the school was often highly praised by the Inspectors. Nonetheless, stone throwing was a particular problem which it would appear was difficult to solve. In one incident, a boy named Higgins was injured and had to be kept away from school for a whole week while he recovered. In the winter of 1902, the school received a visit from the local policeman insisting that the boys did not make slides on the public highway. Later in the same year, in March, the police posted notices asking boys not to steal eggs from nests. Boys, it would appear, would be boys at the turn of the new century.

Frequent complaints were made by local residents about boys indulging in rough behaviour on the way home from school. This often resulted in damage to fences in properties adjacent to the school. The church was also not immune to such visits. In

September 1902 the Reverend Hankey spoke to a number of boys about vandalising trees in the churchyard at St. Luke's. There were also complaints on fairly rare occasions about foul language being audible.

A constantly recurring problem was that of lateness. It is often referred to in the log book kept on a weekly basis by the headmaster. The names of the worst offenders were passed on to the attendance officer whose job it was to check up with parents and find a reason for the late coming. This man also had to deal with those pupils whose attendance rate was giving cause for concern. The accepted method of dealing with pupils who failed to respond was to use the courts to summons the parents of such students.

The name of Henry Gaskin was one that must have come to the attention of the attendance officer. Henry Gaskin did not enjoy a good track record when it came to attendance. Much of this was down no doubt to health problems. The frequent headaches would have meant that he was often absent. Gaskin was frequently ill as a youngster which would also have led to many absences. Outbreaks of contagious diseases may have taken their toll upon Gaskin. An outbreak of scarlet fever in November 1901 may well have added Gaskin to its list of victims. He may also have succumbed to a measles epidemic between May and November of 1902.

Gaskin, on top of this, found it difficult to make friends which may have placed additional pressure on his attendance. This may have been down to his mood swings where one moment he could be very lively whereas the next he could be severely depressed. This would have made other children, not to mention their parents, somewhat wary of such a seemingly strange child.

Gaskin therefore sought a solution to his problems. Sadly, the one he chose was to play truant from school. This was by no means unusual. Truancy is not just a modern day curse upon the education system. Unfortunately, in Gaskin's case it would lead to an incident which undoubtedly affected the rest of his life, and had an impact on the relationship he enjoyed with his family, especially with his father.

Early in 1903, the young Gaskin, a boy named Frank Weaver and his sister Agnes Mary, decided to play truant. The Gaskin family were at this time living in Newhall Street, Cannock. The three youngsters decided to play in a field at the back of the Market Place in Cannock. Near this field were some vans where travelling people lived. One of these vans was inhabited by William Tompkinson, described as an old man, aged around sixty seven. Tompkinson came out of his van and shouted to the three children, "Come with me, all of you". The children, obviously not suspicious went with Tompkinson into his van. After a few minutes, Tompkinson gave Agnes Mary a penny and gave Henry a halfpenny, telling the two boys to go out. Weaver, it would appear, gained nothing from the transaction. Tompkinson then told Agnes that he would give her another penny if she would stay with him in the van. Clearly the alarm bells were not ringing. She was only nine years of age and had probably been told that adults were to be trusted and treated with respect. Her brother also did not appear to be unduly concerned about leaving his sister.

Once the boys had left the events took a more sinister turn. Tompkinson locked the door. Agnes was now obviously worried and asked to go. One can only imagine the horror and panic that must have been going through the terrified mind of this little nine year old girl. Tompkinson would not let her out of the van and carried out an indecent assault upon the innocent girl. This disgusting and perverted act was witnessed by the two boys who had climbed up to the window outside the van. Again one can only imagine the sheer horror of Gaskin seeing his sister abused in this way. Tompkinson then offered Agnes money not to say anything about what had transpired. Clearly the girl and her brother had the common sense to go to their mother. Harriett Gaskin was a formidable woman. Her first reaction was to go round to the van and confront Tompkinson where she threatened to kill him. The next stop was to go to Cannock police where the sorry tale unfolded. The case came to trial at the Magistrates Court on 27th

April 1903. Lord Hatherton, in sentencing the prisoner, Tompkinson, to six months hard labour, regretted that he could not send him to gaol for twice that length of time.

It is almost certain that the young Henry would have borne the blame for this incident. He was eleven, coming twelve, whereas his sister was only nine. Henry's psychological damage would have been just as great as that of his sister, even though she had experienced the humiliation and degradation at the hands of this disgusting man. Henry would have blamed himself for the harm he had allowed to befall his sister. Yet, what is interesting is the absence of the father of the two children. Henry Gaskin senior does not seem to have been involved in the proceedings at any time. His wife, not he, went to see Tompkinson and threatened him. Perhaps what this shows is the delicate balance of the Gaskin family. The father could well have blamed his son completely for what happened to Agnes, and this may have affected the relationship between father and son in the future. To young Henry, just when he needed his father's support, it was not forthcoming. Not for the first time in his life, he probably felt alone with only the love of his mother to rely upon.

A rather depressing sequel to this incident occurred in 1904. On March 27th of that year, William Tompkinson was sent to gaol for a further six months hard labour for a sexual assault on a thirteen year old girl named Bennett, of John Street Chadsmoor. This time the witness was Mrs. Arrowsuch of Newhall Street Cannock, no doubt a neighbour of the Gaskins.

Events now seemed to be taking a further downward turn for the Gaskins. On 21st May 1904, William Williams, a miner living in Newhall Street, Cannock, was summonsed for assaulting Harriet Gaskin. At around three o' clock in the afternoon Harriet was going to the coalhouse when Williams' nephew spoke to her and then went for his uncle. Williams came and threatened to punch Harriet. He then struck her. Williams, it appeared, was the worse for drink, a fact corroborated by a man named Warrington, perhaps one of the two men who pulled Williams away from Harriet Gaskin. The nephew, Arthur, claimed that Mrs. Gaskin had been making allegations about statements his uncle had made about their landlady. Arthur had then gone and told his uncle what had been said resulting in the assault. The magistrates obviously felt that the assault had been provoked or was the result of drink. Either way they decided not to convict Williams but ordered him to pay the costs of some eight shillings. It is again perhaps worthy of note that the name of Henry Joseph Alfred Gaskin is conspicuous by its absence. An intriguing aspect of the case was the reference to letters written by Harriet Gaskin to Williams. These stated that Mrs. Gaskin's husband had forbidden his wife to see or speak to Williams again. This clearly suggests that an affair of some description had taken place between the two. Perhaps this explains the absence of Mr. Gaskin from the proceedings. It may also explain the further souring of relations in the Gaskin family.

The magistrates were not, it would appear, in such an understanding mood a few months later. On 6th July Mary Deakin prosecuted Henry Gaskin, aged twelve but just short of his thirteenth birthday for assault. The magistrates took a rather dim view and fined Henry two shillings and sixpence but with an additional eleven shillings and sixpence in costs. Life was beginning to turn sour for the eldest son of Henry and Harriet Gaskin.

By 1906 the Gaskin family had once more moved house. They were now living at Blencowe's Buildings in Huntington. It was here that on 7th May Harriet Gaskin was summonsed for assaulting Mary Bott. Mary Bott alleged that Harriet Gaskin had come to her house and used offensive language with respect to a table. Harriet Gaskin then punched Mary twice in the stomach. Mrs. Gaskin claimed that she had been good to Mary Bott lending her furniture in the past. This was denied by Mary Bott. The magistrates clearly were more convinced by Mary Bott's evidence and ordered Harriet Gaskin to pay the costs of eight shillings.

Whilst this was serious enough, it paled almost into insignificance compared to the next installment in the life of Henry Thomas Gaskin. The young Gaskin, now some fourteen years of age, had left school and was in need of work. He decided on 15th May to head towards Teddesley in the pursuit of employment. However, Henry did not find work but did manage to get himself into serious trouble. James Moody an engine driver employed at the Littleton Colliery but living at West Chadsmoor said that on the day concerned at about ten fifteen in the morning he took a train to Penkridge. The foreman shunter got off the train and fastened the points with a nut and bolt. At around two in the afternoon he was taking another train to Penkridge when he noticed that the points were half open. He slammed on the brakes and managed to bring the train to a halt only three yards from the points. He found that the nut and bolt had been removed and the points wedged open with cinders from the side of the track. Moody put the line right and continued with his journey. Moody claimed that had the train been heavy he would have been unable to stop in time. William Shepherd the foreman shunter stated that he had fastened the points securely with a nut and a bolt.

Police Constable Knight arrested Gaskin in Huntington and charged him. Gaskin admitted going up the line and taking the nut and bolt off the points and then propping the points open. Gaskin had then gone onto the railway bridge where the line went under the New Penkridge Road, and waited to see what would happen. He claimed that he was sorry but that he had not thought about the possible consequences of his actions.

The magistrates then learned that the father of the young Gaskin was not in court. The sentence was therefore deferred until Henry Joseph Gaskin was present. The court was determined to punish such outrageous conduct by Henry Gaskin junior. The case was adjourned for the attendance of the father at Cannock Police Court.

The fact that Gaskin's father had decided not to attend suggests that he had now washed his hands of his troublesome son. He perhaps felt that as his son was old enough to work , he was old enough to take responsibility for his own actions and more importantly to accept the punishment that went hand in hand with his son's sheer stupidity.

Nonetheless the magistrates had insisted that Gaskin senior should attend and attend he did. On the 28th May, the senior magistrate made it very clear that he considered it to be the parents' responsibility to punish their son. He ordered Henry Gaskin junior to sit down to give his father the opportunity to say what he would do to punish the errant behaviour of his son. At the end of the court, Henry Gaskin senior made it very clear that he was not prepared to pay the very heavy fine of £1 which the magistrates were prepared to accept as settlement of the case. His son had always been troublesome and he had had enough of his son's actions. This was too much for Harriet Gaskin, especially when the magistrates made it very clear that non payment of the fine would result in a prison term. She said that she would not allow her only son to be sent to prison and that she would pay the fine. The Gaskins were now at such odds that a repair to their relationship would be difficult to achieve.

If Mrs. Gaskin hoped that her son would learn a lesson after the very real prospect of imprisonment then she was to be disappointed within a very few short weeks. Henry Thomas Gaskin had succeeded in finding a job at Mr. Lewis Edwards' farm at Huntington. One of his fellow employees was a man named William McDermott, a farm labourer. On 8th July McDermott made a complaint to Police Constable Knight. Knight made enquiries and found the watch McDermott claimed had been stolen was in the possession of a man called Warrington who resided with the parents of Henry Thomas Gaskin at Blencowe's Buildings in Huntington. Warrington obviously told the police officer that the young Gaskin had given him the watch. With this information, Knight visited Hatherton Farm and took Gaskin junior into custody for stealing the watch from the cowhouse. Gaskin's response was typical; he said "I don't know anything about it. I did see a man come here to look for work on Wednesday, perhaps he took it. That's all I know".

McDermott said that he had missed the watch in question from his box where the accused had seen him put it. The watch was extremely valuable being worth over £4. The bench remanded Gaskin for a week with a view to sending him to an Industrial School as he had been in trouble before.

After the remand of one week, Gaskin was brought before the magistrates for sentencing. His age was now given as fifteen. The magistrates were mindful that only a short time before, Gaskin had been dealt with leniently when he had attempted to derail a train on the mineral line between Huntington and Penkridge. Such leniency was not going to be repeated. Gaskin was sentenced to be sent to Saltley Industrial School until he was nineteen years of age and that the court required the parents of the boy to make a contribution towards his maintenance. Gaskin's claim that he was "very sorry" clearly failed to cut any ice with the magistrates.

This would have been a devastating blow, in particular to his mother, Harriet. Perhaps to his father it merely confirmed that what he had said before was now vindicated. Both parents would have been even more disheartened on 27th August when a maintenance order was set at three shillings per week. A fine of a further ten shillings was also imposed by the court, adding insult to injury as far as Henry Gaskin senior was concerned. Gaskin claimed that the court had miscalculated his earnings. The court stated that his earnings were £1 13s 3d per week. Gaskin claimed that this included over time which equated to eight working days. Nonetheless the will of the court prevailed. Gaskin would have to pay.

However, Gaskin had the last word. On 12th August 1907 he managed to overturn the Magistrates' order and, at a cost of four shillings, had the amount that he was expected to contribute to his son at Saltley, reduced from three shillings per week to half of that amount. As far as Henry Joseph Gaskin was concerned this was a moral victory.

Nonetheless, the fact remained that his son Henry Thomas Gaskin would spend the next four years of his life at Saltley. This would deprive Mrs. Gaskin of her only son for four years. The Scouts and the Cannock Brass Band had also lost the flamboyant skills of their leading drummer. It was, for Gaskin, an opportunity to learn from his mistakes, to improve his skills with future job prospects in mind and he would also have a chance to extend his education.

## Chapter Five

# A CHANCE TO REFORM

Saltley Industrial School or Reformatory had been serving the community since the mid 19th century. Its purpose was to take criminal boys from all parts of the kingdom and attempt to reform their lives and offer them an alternative to crime and an opportunity to become useful members of the Empire. The school was under local management and was reliant on subscription for much of its funding. As a private institution it charged payments for "custody and maintenance".

When Gaskin entered the gates of the school in late 1906, he may or may not have been aware of the officers of the reformatory. The President was C. A. Smith-Ryland, who was assisted by two Vice-Presidents, namely the Right Honourable, the Earl of Shrewsbury and Talbot and the Right Honourable, the Lord Mayor of Birmingham. The Honourary Chaplain at this time was the Reverend Honourable J. G. Adderley.

Gaskin would have been more aware and indeed familiar with the Superintendent of Saltley. This was Stephen Arnold who had been in day to day charge for a number of years. He was ably assisted by the Matron, Mrs. Fish, who had been at Saltley since 1885 when her late husband had been the Superintendent. It is clear from records that both Stephen Arnold and Mrs. Fish were respected and well liked by many of the boys who passed through the school. There are many letters from former pupils of the school who had gone on to lead successful lives who were obviously proud of the school and grateful to Arnold and Fish. Indeed many of these boys saw the two of them as parents.

This is not to say that either Stephen Arnold or Mrs. Fish were a soft touch. The discipline at Saltley was firm but fair, a point often referred to in letters from former pupils. Perhaps it may be opportune to consider the routine that Gaskin would have faced.

From Monday to Saturday, the day began at 5:45 in the morning when boys had to rise and make their beds. At 6:00 a roll call was taken before washing. Prayers were made at 6:15 lasting for 15 minutes when all standards went to school and band practice. At 7:00 all boys attended Industrial Employment for 30 minutes, followed by recreation in the playground before breakfast. Only 20 minutes were given to eating breakfast which was followed by 10 minutes recreation again in the playground. At 8:30 the "A" Division of boys were sent to the formal school rooms whilst the "B" Division went to Industrial Employment. This would last for the whole morning until, at 12:30, the boys would have to wash and relax before dinner at 1:00. Again only 20 minutes was devoted to eating followed by a further 25 minutes in the playground for recreation. At 1:45 the "A" and "B" Divisions changed around from their morning activities, again taking up the afternoon until 5:45 when the boys washed and prepared for supper. Once more 20 minutes was given for eating followed by an hour and 20 minutes for recreation. At 7:40 a roll call was taken followed by prayers and boys had to be in bed by 8:00.

This was a full day by any standards and would have come as a shock to many of the boys to begin with. However, the routine would have become something of a comfort to many of those who were not used to a structured lifestyle.

Sundays were slightly more relaxed. The day did not begin until 6:15 when again the boys had to rise and make beds. At 6:30 a roll call was taken followed by washing. At 7:00 there was a general lesson on Collect and the Gospel text for the day and then 30 minutes of prayers before breakfast. Recreation began at 9:00 and lasted for half an hour before a similar amount of time devoted to Religious Instruction. At 10:00 the boys had to prepare for church which lasted from 10:15 until 1:00. Dinner lasted for 20 minutes which was then followed by recreation for an hour and 25 minutes. From 2:25 until 4:00, Sunday School was attended at the end of which the boys had an hour for recreation and to prepare for tea, taken at 5:00. Boys were then free, within the confines of the school, before bed again at 8:00.

The meals at Saltley were rather repetitious but nutritious and filling. For many of the boys concerned it would undoubtedly have been the first time that they had received regular, filling and healthy meals. Breakfast consisted of one pint of milk porridge together with 7-10 ounces of bread. Dinner depended on the day and followed a strict rota. On Monday 8-10 ounces of bread was served with 2 and a half ounces of cheese with salad. Tuesday meant 6 ounces of meat, with bread and vegetables. On Wednesday the boys had one pint of pea soup and 7 ounces of bread. Thursday consisted of between 12 and 20 ounces of suet pudding served with stewed fruit. Friday repeated Tuesday and Saturday was the same as Wednesday. Sunday was probably seen as a treat to some extent; suet pudding served with treacle and sultanas.

Supper on all days was one pint of tea, coffee or cocoa, 7-10 ounces of bread with dripping or butter, with salad in the summer. Greater quantities were given between 1st November and 31st March.

The facilities at Saltley were very good indeed and were designed to get the best out of the pupils and to make them proud of achievement. All boys were drilled by Mr. Tozer in the use of fire extinguishers. Religious Instruction, including the Sunday School, was undertaken by students of Saltley Diocesan Training College. Lessons were given in agriculture, drawing, tailoring and shoe making, along with farm and garden instruction. Attempts were also made to improve the basic skills of reading and writing as many of the boys had learning difficulties. This gave rise to frequent inspections when the overall standard of education was consistently recorded as good.

The sporting and recreational facilities at Saltley were excellent and extremely varied. Fitness was seen as being of the utmost importance. Boys used dumb bells, Indian clubs and parallel bars to obtain strength and stamina and to improve muscle tone. Maze running was also popular. Selected boys were taken to Small Heath baths for swimming. There was also a series of three one day outings and sundry concerts and entertainments which were provided by the boys. Music was a very important part of the experience of the boys. The school band was some 27 strong with a further 30 boys learning to play instruments. Gaskin's expertise as a drummer would have been put to good use in the band. It may also be that whilst he was at Saltley, he was introduced to the piano for the first time.

Competitive sport was also crucial to the boys and was part of the school's attempt to raise their sense of worth and achievement. Football was very popular and in 1906 the school team enjoyed 13 wins out of 28 games. Indeed the school was considered to be in the front rank when it came to swimming and sports generally.

In 1906, the high standard of the school was maintained. 34 boys were admitted to Saltley, which raised the number to 99. Some 28 of these were out in employment on licence. Over the year a total of 31 boys were discharged and 27 of these went into employment. This is a remarkable testimony to Stephen Arnold and his staff. Three boys had emigrated to Canada on release and one boy enlisted, quite a common path for ex Saltley boys.

The same year saw the grant for each boy raised by 6d. This meant that a minimum of 2s 6d was expected per inmate from the contributing authorities. Some of this was spent on a new clothing requirement, including Sunday suits of blue beaver cloth and new nightshirts for each boy.

The breakdown of geographical areas for the inmates of 1906 makes interesting reading. Thirteen of them, including Henry Gaskin, were from Staffordshire. There was one boy from each of Glamorganshire, Caernarvonshire, Worcestershire, Leicestershire

31

and one boy from Margate. Derbyshire provided two boys, Cardiff four, Liverpool four and Birmingham four, with a further two coming from Burton.

Five of these boys were aged 12, nine were aged 13, twelve were aged 14 and eight were aged 15. Only three of these boys could read and write well. Twenty four could read and write imperfectly and seven could read and write a little. Only seven of the boys had no previous convictions, eleven of them had one previous conviction, fourteen had two previous convictions, one had three previous convictions and one had four previous convictions. Presumably, Gaskin was the one boy with three previous convictions against his name. Of further interest with regard to the thirty four boys admitted in 1906, was the fact that twenty eight of them had both parents living, including Gaskin; two had experienced the death of their mother and four, the death of their father.

In 1907, Gaskin would have had another thirty boys to get to know, if he so chose. This meant that the total number of inmates had risen to one hundred and one. Twenty three of these were out on licence, working prior to possible release. Thirty three boys had been discharged and of these, twenty five had managed to find employment, again with the outstanding help of Saltley. Four inmates had decided to emigrate to Canada and two chose to enlist into the armed services. No mention is made of the remaining two boys but as Stephen Arnold had previously stated in his annual reports to the Board of the school, some boys sadly chose to return to the very people who had, often, got them into trouble in the first place.

1907 also saw the establishment of rifle practice at Saltley. This proved to be very popular and indeed a team of boys from the school won the Challenge Cup in open competition with other Home Office schools. The school remained well to the fore on all sports. Members of the Army Class of the school had progressed so well that they were able to sit for the Education Certificate.

A dentist was appointed at the school in 1908, a Mr. E. Trevor-Williams. This would benefit the dental health of the inmates. A new Medical Officer, Mr. Feast, also joined the staff. The facilities of the school again began to show improvement with a new gymnasium planned and a miniature rifle range set up at the school. The rifles were provided by Mr. J. E. Haskins with Mr. Alderman Bayliss ensuring that ammunition was available. This was almost certainly a facility used by Gaskin and would have unfortunate consequences in his life. The name of the school was also changed to Norton Boys' Home.

Life had not stood still for the rest of the Gaskin family whist Henry junior had been at Saltley. The fascination with the legal system continued. On the 2nd April 1907 Harriet Gaskin put in another appearance before the magistrates at Cannock on a charge of assault upon Maud Webb. Just for good measure, Mrs. Gaskin lodged a counter charge against Mrs. Webb. The Gaskin family were now living at Huntington Wharf and what transpired between the two women reads almost like farce. Mrs. Webb emptied a bucket full of ashes on the ground, presumably to soak up water on the yard shared by the two properties. Harriet Gaskin for some reason objected to this and picked up the ashes. Webb then threw the ashes down again to be followed by Mrs. Gaskin getting a bucket full of water from the scullery and throwing this upon the ashes. Mrs. Webb then grabbed Mrs. Gaskin by the hair and kicked her three times. This was the version of events offered by Mrs. Gaskin to the magistrates.

Mrs. Webb gave another version. She claimed that she had thrown down the ashes for the sole purpose of soaking up water. Mrs. Gaskin had then thrown water all over the ashes and indeed over Mrs. Webb. A man named Husselbee said he saw Mrs. Gaskin on top of Mrs. Webb while Mrs. Gaskin's daughter, Agnes Mary, was kicking the poor Mrs. Webb. To add insult to injury this took place on Mrs. Webb's property. The magistrates dismissed the case against Mrs. Webb; after all, her evidence did have some independent corroboration. Harriet Gaskin was left to pay the costs which amounted to some 14 shillings. Clearly Harriet Gaskin seemed hell bent on showing a bad example to her errant son.

This was followed on the 6th August 1907 with an appearance by Henry Gaskin senior before the magistrates at Cannock. He had been summonsed by Samuel Shaw, the school attendance officer, on a charge of neglecting to send a child to school. The case was adjourned until the 19th when after due consideration it was dismissed by the magistrates; a victory for Mr. Gaskin.

An interesting episode took place in 1908. Henry Gaskin junior must have been on a visit from the Reformatory at Saltley. On 27th July a dog, owned by James Lees, a dealer from Walsall Wood, bit him and his father informed Police Constable Williams. Indeed, a fortnight previously, the same dog had bitten Henry Gaskin senior. The defendant, Mr. Lees, was let off the fine and costs of £1 8s 9d on condition of destroying the dog. This was yet another victory for Henry Gaskin senior in the courts. However, it was literally a painful reminder of the realities of life for his son.

Once again at Cannock Magistrates Court on 13th April 1909 a member of the Gaskin family found themselves accused of assault. Sarah Poole claimed that Henry Gaskin junior had hit her on the 3rd April. Presumably Gaskin, referred to as Harry for the first time, must have been on release from Saltley. Either that or it was a case of mistaken identity because the magistrates struck out the case. Perhaps the reputation of Henry Thomas Gaskin was beginning to go ahead of him.

There was some good news for the family in April 1910. On the 23rd of that month, Agnes Mary Gaskin, now aged 17, married William Warrington, a 34 year old lamp cleaner. The marriage was conducted by F. L. Ashworth at St. Luke's, Cannock, the event witnessed by the bride's father, and by Clara Cadman. Whether Harry was able to attend the happy event is not recorded. The happy couple celebrated the birth of a daughter, Eleanor, by the end of the year.

Still the courts had not finished with the Gaskins. Harriet was clearly having problems keeping her hands to herself, for on the 3rd October 1910, she was summonsed by Caroline Husselbee for assault. Again the events unfolded at Huntington Wharf and again the court found against Mrs. Gaskin. Whether this had been simmering since the Webb incident is anyone's guess. After all Henry Husselbee had given evidence against Harriet Gaskin on that occasion. A fine of 2s 6d together with 12s 6d costs was levied against Mrs. Gaskin. She was given ten days to pay. A fascinating entry in the record is that Harriet Gaskin had cancer. There is no other evidence to verify this entry. Perhaps Mrs. Gaskin was trying to gain the sympathy of the magistrates.

Gaskin had been sentenced to serve at Norton Boys' Home until his 19th birthday. This meant that his discharge was in 1910. In that year a record 35 boys had been admitted to the school, increasing the roll to 107. 36 boys were out on licence to local employers. Gaskin was one of the 35 boys discharged, 32 of whom were placed into employment.

Stephen Arnold had a number of contacts that he must have built up over the years. He wanted to help his boys, as much as was possible, to put their past behind them and start a new life. Arnold was only too aware that Gaskin was approaching his nineteenth birthday and so he arranged for Harry to visit the recruiting office in Birmingham in early July 1910. The visit was successful for Henry Thomas Gaskin, who, with the support of his father, was recruited into the West Yorkshire Regiment as a Private soldier. This would have met the hopes of Arnold and of his father. Harry was to make a new start away from the temptations of his former life. He passed his medical with flying colours. He was now just over 5 feet 6 in height, with a fresh complexion, grey eyes and brown hair. An interesting identifying feature referred to is the existence of three pitted scars on the back of his neck, perhaps the legacy of the dog attack in 1908.

Sadly the new opportunity turned into a disaster. Arnold had given an excellent testimonial for Gaskin, stating that he was a sober, honest and hard working young man, who had learned from his previous mistakes. On the basis of this he joined his Regiment on 8th July 1910. Within a matter of hours after arriving at the Depot he was charged with assaulting a fellow Private. This was swiftly followed by a second charge of theft. Gaskin received 56 days in the glasshouse for both misdemeanours on 8th October and was discharged from the Army in disgrace on 11th November 1910.

Harry Gaskin's life was now in tatters. He had not only let himself down; he had failed the kindness and help shown to him by Stephen Arnold and had also thrown away the chance to re-establish his relationship with his own father. Gaskin would have felt, not for the first time in his existence that he was very much alone against the world.

Just as the Talbot family would have been glad to see the back of the first decade of the new century, then so too would the Gaskins. After all their only son had gone off the rails in such a way as to warrant time served at Saltley Reformatory. They had also had the horror of Agnes Mary suffering a sexual assault. Harriet Gaskin had become a familiar figure at the local magistrates' court and seemed to be having immense problems keeping her temper under control. Perhaps the next decade would bring better luck and an improvement in fortune.

*Chapter Six*

# THE TALBOTS MOVE FORWARD

After a difficult, often traumatic decade, 1910 seemed to be offering a fresh start for the Talbot family. On 9th May at St. Peter's Parish Church, Hednesford, Abner William Talbot, now 21 years of age, married Sarah Ann Day, also 21. He was described as a bachelor, she, in that quaint phrase, as a spinster. Abner's profession is given as a coal miner and it is believed that he was employed by the West Cannock Colliery Company at its Number Three Pit. The address for both bride and groom is given as Platt Street, Hightown, which would suggest that the happy couple were residing with the bride's family. The father of the groom was listed as Henry Charles Talbot and that of the bride as George Henry Day, who sadly had not lived to see his daughter married. The ceremony was performed by William Quibell, the Vicar of Hednesford and was witnessed by Jesse Bowater and Phoebe Susannah Bagnall.

Whether the address of bride and groom suggests that perhaps the union was not universally welcomed by the Talbot family is after this expanse of time a matter of mere conjecture. It was, though, a change of fortune. Abner appeared to have put his earlier indiscretions behind him and was now in employment and with the additional responsibility of a new bride to contend with. In these circumstances, families often rally round and the couple probably had the blessing and support of both families.

Certainly, there would have been joy expressed in 1911 with the announcement that Abner and Sarah Ann were expecting their first child. The birth of Emma Elizabeth Talbot took place at 67, Brindley Heath on the 28th April 1912. The fact that the couple had moved to within a few doors of the rest of the Talbot family would clearly support the view that any rift was now fully healed. The baptism of the new baby took place at St. Peter's on the 29th May 1912.

This happy event was followed by more good news for the Talbots. On December 21st 1912, Mary Ann Talbot, now aged twenty, married Francis Dando, a twenty year old miner. Again the ceremony took place at St. Peter's Church and was carried out by William Quibell. The proceedings were witnessed by Earnest Dando and Emma Bullock. The address of the bride was given as 72, Brindley Heath, Mary Ann still living with her parents. The address of the groom was stated as 78, Brindley Heath. The two families were obviously near neighbours and probably friends. Both of the fathers of the couple, Henry Charles Talbot and Alfred Dando were miners. Presumably Francis Dando would have known of the problems that Mary Ann had experienced earlier in her life. It is to his credit that he was willing to accept what had gone before and would suggest that the bond between the two was a strong one.

Further happiness was extended to the Talbot family in 1913, when Mary Ann and Francis Dando announced the birth of their first child. The baby, named Earnest, after the father's brother, who had been one of the witnesses to their marriage, was born on 20th February with the christening taking place at St. Peter's on 7th May. The address of the Dando family was given as 77, Brindley Heath. As was common at the time the Dandos had not ventured far from their roots. This ceremony was performed by J. H. Darby.

This had been preceded by the birth, on 31st January of Rose Hannah Bagnall. She was the first child of William Bagnall and his wife Phoebe Susannah, who had been one of the witnesses at the marriage of Abner and Sarah Ann Talbot. The christening took place on 26th February 1913. The new family lived at 75, Brindley Heath and so the christening would have been celebrated by friends and neighbours many of whom were related to each other in some way. The first years of the new decade were going swimmingly for the Talbot family and their friends and relations.

The same appeared to hold true for the Gaskin family. There is no record of any appearances before the magistrates or of any newspaper entry to denote otherwise. Henry Thomas Gaskin was at work in the colliery and it would seem had become a member of the Hednesford branch of the Boy Scouts' Association. The family had moved to St John's Street in Cannock in the meantime.

At around this time in Hednesford the new picture house opened in Anglesey Street. In order to mark the occasion a fancy dress carnival was held. This may have been the background to one of Gaskin's most remembered escapades. Gaskin rode into Hednesford on a horse dressed as a native American. This caused quite a stir and remained in popular memory, becoming over time part of Hednesford folklore. As time passed Gaskin was credited with having a gun of some description, but this may have been added as a result of later events. Again the Gaskin family seemed to have turned the corner in the first years of the new decade.

Unfortunately, for both the Talbot family and the Gaskin household new problems and tragedies were just around the corner. The birth of Emma Elizabeth to Abner and Sarah Ann Talbot was no doubt a happy event. Imagine then the sense of desolation that would have been felt by the untimely death of Sarah Ann, aged 25, on the 11th August 1912. She died from a combination of pneumonia, asthenia and heart failure. The death occurred at 67, Brindley Heath and Abner was present as his wife died. The whole family would have been hit very hard by this sad news.

For the Gaskin family too, 1912 would bring its problems. Henry Thomas Gaskin seemed to have settled down to a new life and to have learned from his earlier experiences; events were about to show, however, that this was a false dawn. Stephen Arnold had always maintained that inmates who returned to their roots were most likely to re-offend. Arnold was about to be proved right.

*Chapter Seven*

# DEMANDING MONEY

On Monday 4th March 1912, Jessie Gladys Darby, a domestic servant from Hednesford, was walking along the Old Hednesford Road towards Cannock to meet her boyfriend. This was about 7:15 in the evening and thus would have been quite dark. She was approached by a man who was wearing a dark coloured cloth over his face and had his cap pulled down low over his forehead. The man was holding some kind of firearm and demanded money, stating that if she screamed, he would shoot. Jessie Darby was probably terrified out of her wits but managed to stammer out that she had no money. Although frightened, she did have the presence of mind to offer her watch as an alternative to hard cash. The man was not interested in hard goods and then grabbed the young woman by the arm, saying "I don't want your money, come with me". The girl at this point saw her boyfriend heading towards them and imparted this information to her assailant, who ran off, in the direction of Cannock.

This was a disturbing case. The use of a firearm, whether or not it was loaded, was a serious offence. The assault also raised questions. If the robber did not want her money or her watch, then what was his motive for dragging her towards waste land off the Old Hednesford Road?

The following evening, Tuesday 5th March, a young girl of 16 years of age, Mona Mary Bennion, was walking with a friend when the couple were approached at around 7:30 in the evening. Again the description and method of crime were exactly the same. The man had a dark coloured cloth covering his face and his cap pulled low over his forehead. A firearm was again used. This time the attack took place at Commonside, Chadsmoor. The girl had no money, and this time the assailant ran off.

On Wednesday 6th March, at around 11:00 in the morning Mary Jellyman, the wife of Ebenezer Jellyman, of St. John's Road, Cannock was riding her bicycle down the Penkridge Road, towards the village. As she approached Mansty Bridge, she dismounted her cycle and began to push it up the incline. She noticed a man, also with a cycle, who proceeded to place his cycle across the road crosswise thus stopping Mary from going on. It was at this point that Mrs. Jellyman noticed that the man had a dark coloured cloth over his face and that his cap was pulled low over his forehead. She also noticed that the man had some kind of pistol in his hand. Mary Jellyman also noticed that the man had a scout's axe; she recognised the string that passed through the handle of the implement, protruding out of his overcoat pocket. The man demanded money and threatened to shoot unless payment was forthcoming.

Mary Jellyman sensibly decided to hand over her cash. She did not know whether the man would or would not carry out his threat. She did not know whether or not the pistol was loaded or able to fire. She gave the man between three and four shillings. The man only took one shilling and then got on his cycle and rode off towards Cannock. Mrs. Jellyman noticed two other men also on cycles and did not know whether the man had accomplices.

Shortly afterwards the man was seen waiting in Mansty Lane by Herbert Mansfield Whitehead, a surveyor employed by Cannock Rural District Council. He saw the man sitting astride his cycle watching him. After Whitehead had passed, he got on his cycle and pedalled furiously towards Cannock. Mr. Whitehead was also sure that the two men seen by Mrs. Jellyman also headed towards Cannock. Mr. Whitehead saw Mrs. Jellyman in a somewhat distressed state and suggested that she make her way back home and inform the police. This is precisely what Mrs. Jellyman did.

The police were already aware that a dangerous man had committed at least two similar crimes in the district. However, it would seem that Mary Jellyman was very observant, perhaps aided by clear daylight. She passed on her description to Superintendent John Campbell. Mrs. Jellyman may have had suspicions of her own that she also shared with the police. She may have recognised more than the scout's axe. Perhaps the cycle was reminiscent of one ridden by a young man who also lived in St. John's Road. She may have even recognised the overcoat worn by her attacker.

Therefore, before the day was out Superintendent Campbell, along with Sergeant O' Leary was knocking on the door of 63, St John's Road, Cannock. They had called to ask questions of Henry Thomas Gaskin. Gaskin at first denied having been anywhere near Mansty Bridge but then admitted the crime. He was arrested and taken before Cannock magistrates on 9th March 1912, charged with demanding money with menaces on 6th March. In the light of the seriousness of the crime, Gaskin was remanded in the cells until 11th March.

At Cannock on 11th March, Gaskin, referred to as a labourer working at the West Cannock Colliery and aged twenty, faced three charges. For the case involving Jessie Darby he was charged with assault with intent to rob. The same charge was levied in the case involving Mona Bennion. In the case on the 6th March, with Mary Jellyman, Gaskin was charged with demanding mòney with menaces. For the latter offence Gaskin was fined 1s with 8s 6d costs. For the other cases the costs came to £1 13s 6d and 16s respectively. However, if Gaskin momentarily thought that he had escaped lightly he was very much mistaken. For the magistrates then remanded Gaskin to appear at the next Quarter Sessions to be held at Stafford. In the meantime he would remain in custody.

These incidents do throw up some questions. The motivation of Gaskin is not immediately clear. If it was robbery then why did he not take money from Mona Bennion and why did he refuse the watch offered by Jessie Darby? Indeed, if robbery was the motive then it appears incomprehensible that on being given between three and four shillings by Mary Jellyman, he only took one shilling. Perhaps there was a more sinister reason behind Gaskin's actions. After all, in the case of Jessie Darby he had said "I don't want your money, come with me". Did Gaskin have a sexual motive for the assault? Was he thwarted by the timely arrival of Miss Darby's boyfriend?

An interesting observation in the Jellyman case is the location of the incident. The bridge at Mansty was the very same bridge that Gaskin, then aged 14, had stood on when waiting to see what would happen to the mineral train after he had unscrewed the plates from the points. Again here, the robbery angle would not appear to fit the facts completely. If so then why not take all of the money? Perhaps it was some macabre joke, a test of nerve and courage. Whatever the reason, the police and the magistrates saw the case as being disturbing and serious.

At the Quarter Sessions at Stafford, on the 13th April 1912, Henry Thomas Gaskin appeared before the judge to answer the three charges that had been brought against him at Cannock in March. After listening carefully to the evidence, and no doubt being mindful of Gaskin's previous record, the judge decided that a custodial sentence was appropriate. Henry Thomas Gaskin was sentenced to serve twelve months in prison at Stafford Gaol. When the judgement had been delivered all attention was then focused upon the public gallery where a woman became hysterical. She was screaming and sobbing "My son, my only son", and on leaving the gallery she fell down heavily. Clearly Harriet Gaskin was having difficulty coping with the realisation that her only son was guilty of a series of very serious crimes. She asked to be allowed to go to her son, but this natural request was ignored by the court officials and the police. Mrs. Gaskin was guided out of the courtroom where her pitiful cries could be heard for some time afterwards. Henry Thomas Gaskin would not have been able to hear them. He would have already made the short journey from the Guildhall in Stafford where the trial took place to the cell in Stafford Gaol from where he had come that morning. It is not recorded whether or not his father, Henry Joseph Gaskin attended the hearing.

## Chapter Eight

# MARRIAGE AND PRISON

Henry Thomas Gaskin served his sentence and was released early in 1913. He went back to live with his parents at St John's Road, Cannock perhaps against the wishes of his father. It is feasible that Gaskin senior was willing, or at least had been persuaded, to give his son another chance. The younger Gaskin then went back to the West Cannock Colliery Company and pleaded for his old job.

Gaskin must have been blessed with some charm or at the very least was highly regarded by his erstwhile employers. For, amazingly, he was set on again, not as a labourer, but this time as a horse driver. This was a responsible and crucial task in a pit at that time. Pit ponies were used to pull heavily laden coal trucks from the coal face to the pit shaft where the trucks were taken up to the surface to be unloaded for washing and grading, prior to distribution for sale.

Unfortunately, Gaskin's bad luck had not left him at the gates of Stafford Gaol. On the 17th March 1913, Gaskin was charged by the Colliery for a breach of the rules. Gaskin appeared in front of the magistrates at Cannock on a charge of negligence, by not carefully conveying coal tubs at West Cannock Colliery Number Three Pit. Gaskin told the court that he had told the "nipper" to take the block out and as a result of this action the tubs had run fifty to sixty yards pinning a poor pit pony and crushing it to death.

The nipper, Leonard Shannon, a young lad of only 15, confirmed the account offered by Gaskin. When Gaskin had been asked what had happened by William Hale, a fireman at the Colliery, he had replied "I don't know". A fairly typical Gaskin response when confronted by responsibility for his actions. Gaskin then went on to show a philosophical or perhaps even fatalistic side of his nature. He claimed that "something told me coming along the road tonight that there was something going to happen".

Gaskin was found not guilty of wilful neglect by the magistrates, but that did not mean that he escaped without censure. The magistrates told him that he should have checked the chain himself before instructing the nipper to take off the block. As a result he had to pay the costs of 14s 8d. Rather an unwelcome reintroduction to the world of work and to life outside prison.

Yet on a personal level, life was seemingly improving for Henry Gaskin. At some point, early in 1913, Gaskin would have announced that he intended to get married. His bride to be was Elizabeth Talbot, whose family lived at 72, Brindley Heath, Hednesford. By all accounts, it would appear that Elizabeth had developed into a lively and outgoing young woman. Her engagement to a quiet and somewhat notorious young man may well have raised one or two eyebrows around Cannock and Hednesford.

However, this spark of liveliness may well have been what Gaskin found to his liking, for Lizzie Talbot was only moderately attractive if her photographs are any guide. She was a small, slight woman of around five feet two in height. Gaskin was a good looking, powerfully built man and as such it is not hard to see what Lizzie found attractive. Perhaps Gaskin's very notoriety was also exciting for Lizzie. Her own family had faced many brushes with authority and so Gaskin may have appeared as a kindred spirit.

Where they had first met is not known. Perhaps they were introduced by her elder brother, Abner, who worked at the West Cannock Colliery Number Three Pit along with Gaskin. We do not know what the respective parents felt about the impending wedding.

It is interesting to note that at the time of their wedding the address for both bride and groom was given as 63, St. John's Road, Cannock, the home of Mr. and Mrs. Gaskin.

Perhaps this was down to the simple matter of room. The household at Brindley Heath was already overcrowded. The Gaskins may have welcomed Elizabeth into their house in order to help their soon to be in laws.

Of greater significance, was the fact that Elizabeth was pregnant. This may well have hastened the process, and hence a rather short engagement would have been essential. The date chosen for the wedding was 20th July 1913, at St. Luke's Parish Church, Cannock. Gaskin's age is given as 21; he was just 2 days away from his 22nd birthday and that of his wife as 20, although she was actually 18. He is described as a bachelor and his wife as a spinster. Gaskin's occupation is listed as a miner. Elizabeth it would seem had no job at that time, although she had worked briefly in service, a common enough occurrence at that time. Both of the couples' fathers are noted on the certificate. Gaskin senior described as a stoker and Talbot as a miner.

The ceremony was conducted by the Vicar of Cannock, T. S. Price and was witnessed by Florence Maud Westwood and H. Gaskin. Whether this was his mother or father is not clear as they shared the same initial for their respective forenames. The signatures of the happy couple make a clear contrast. Gaskin's is in bold and confident copper plate handwriting whereas that of his wife is that of a person to whom writing did not come easily.

It would appear that shortly after the wedding the couple moved to a small apartment near to the Talbot family in Brindley Heath. Everything on the face of it was going well. Gaskin was now a married man, and about to discover the added responsibility of parenthood. The marriage, whilst it may have created an initial stir, would appear to have been welcomed by the two families. His wife and her outgoing personality may just have been what the taciturn Gaskin needed.

Just as things were going well, however, events were soon to take a marked turn for the worse. The new baby was born on 10th December 1912, at 80, Brindley Heath. The birth being helped by a neighbour of the Talbot family. Elizabeth, as a new mother, may have had problems feeding her new baby, as one of her breasts did not produce sufficient milk. The new baby would also have added to the costs of the new family. Either, or both, of these problems could well have triggered off a new wave of crime from her husband.

Whatever the reason, Henry Thomas Gaskin entered upon a series of crimes that would have an impact on his life and on those related to him. The first of this spree was on the night of 20th /21st November 1913. Gaskin entered the premises of Isaac William Bate, a beerhouse keeper who lived and worked on the Rugeley Road, Hednesford. Bate had locked up his premises at around 11:30pm on the night of the 20th November. He had then gone up to bed. At around 5:00 the next morning, he had been awoken by the sound of someone outside the shop window. When he went downstairs he found that the window had been broken and the curtain moved aside. The shop door was propped open by the weights from the scales and was now unbolted. The money drawer had been taken out of the counter and placed under the window outside. Five shillings in money had been taken from the drawer along with bundles of laces, two jars of jam and a can of condensed milk.

These last two items were seen in the apartment that the Gaskins rented in Brindley Heath from Mary and William Morris on the 23rd November. Mrs. Elizabeth Gaskin had told Mrs. Morris that the jam and milk had been given to them by her husband's mother, the previous night.

Four days later Gaskin was back on the streets at the sort of hour when most other people were asleep. On 25th November, he entered the premises of Edward Coombs, a general grocer of Church Street, Cannock. Sarah Coombs, a daughter of the shop owner had locked up and made everything safe at 9:00pm. She had then gone up to bed an hour later. At around 4:45am she was awoken by a light shining in the shop downstairs. Sarah called out thinking that it was her father. On receiving no reply she got out of bed and saw the shadow of a man. She called her father and the two of them made their way downstairs. The sight that greeted them was a lamp burning on the door mat, a ransacked chest of drawers and a rifled till which had 2 shillings and 5 pence missing from it. A large pane of glass had been broken and then a hole big enough to allow a man to enter had been made in the glass. The back door had then been opened and left ajar. Gaskin was obviously thorough enough to make an emergency exit in case he was disturbed. Sadly he was not careful enough to wear gloves and he had left a thumb print on a piece of broken glass.

The crime spree had not yet finished and on the next venture Gaskin had company in the shape of his new brothers in law, Abner and Uriah Talbot. Abner was not a real stranger to the world of crime but his brother would appear to have kept himself out of trouble since his childhood.

Nonetheless, on 17th December 1913 the three men had travelled the short distance to Rugeley. Here they had stolen a counterpane from John Wood of Sandy Lane in the town most associated with the crimes of Palmer the Poisoner. It would seem that the counterpane was then pledged by Mrs. Talbot.

Four days later the two Talbot brothers were once again involved in crime. This time they received a stolen turkey which had been taken from Henry Renshaw. Christmas was just around the corner and the Talbot household wanted to make sure that they had a bird to grace their table.

Part of the motivation for these crimes may well have been the impending marriage of Abner Talbot, for whom the year was ending on a happier note, after the trauma following the death of his first wife Sarah Ann. On Christmas Eve, 1913, Abner married Elsie May Belward, a twenty one year old spinster. The groom's father is listed on the certificate, but there is no mention of the father of the bride. The ceremony was performed by William Quibell at St. Peter's Church and was witnessed by Francis Dando, another brother in law of the groom, and Maria Jane Clare. The wedding would almost certainly have been attended by Harry and Lizzie Gaskin.

The Gaskin/Talbot crime wave abated for the Christmas season of goodwill but shortly into the New Year began again. This time it would appear that Gaskin was once more by himself.

The 14th January 1914 had begun as a happy day for the Gaskins. They had travelled from their apartment in Brindley Heath to St. Luke's Parish Church in Cannock. Here the first child of Harry and Lizzie Gaskin was baptised, being given the names Arthur Henry. The service was performed by T. S. Price, the vicar of Cannock.

Yet within a few hours Gaskin was back to his life of crime. Mary Jones of Mount Street, Hednesford took in washing to supplement her income. On that day she had washed a counterpane and two blankets belonging to John Thomas Harrison, also of Mount Street. The clothing was on the line at 6:30pm but had disappeared an hour later. Harry Gaskin was seen by Jane Ellen Jones of Brindley Heath carrying a large bundle of clothes.

On the 15th January 1914, the Gaskins left the apartment rented from Mrs. Morris and moved to another apartment on Longford Lane Bridgtown. It was here, on the 16th January, that the police in the shape of Sergeant O' Leary and P. C. Barratt of Cannock Constabulary, paid Harry Gaskin a visit. They found him lying on a sofa with a blanket wrapped around him. Barratt went upstairs and discovered another blanket and a counterpane. When charged with the theft Gaskin declared, "I stole them because I wanted some money. I was hard up". When confronted by Barratt for the robbery at Bates' beerhouse, Gaskin replied, "Quite correct".

Gaskin was remanded in custody for seven days at Stafford Gaol and while he was there his finger prints were taken on 21st January and sent to Chief Inspector Charles Collins at New Scotland Yard. Collins was in charge of the finger print section and had been involved with this new branch of evidence since 1901, becoming an expert in the process. Collins compared the prints with those the enterprising P. C. Heath had taken from the broken pane of glass taken from the shop window of Mr. Coombs.

The finger prints were found to be a match. This evidence was backed up with a confession from Gaskin.

Gaskin was sent back to Cannock Magistrates' Court on the 26th January 1914. He was accompanied in the dock by his two brothers in law, Abner and Uriah Talbot, who had also been arrested and charged. For their crimes the Talbot brothers were dealt with separately. Abner was clearly seen as the bad apple and was sentenced to two terms of three months in prison, to be served concurrently. Uriah was discharged on both counts.

For Gaskin there was no leniency. He was sent to Stafford Gaol to await the next Quarter Sessions. These took place on Thursday 5th February and Gaskin pleaded guilty to the burglary of Isaac William Bates' premises. Gaskin also pleaded guilty to similar charges from Cannock Police. He admitted thirteen other offences and asked for these to be taken into consideration. Whether this was correct it is not clear. It may account for Gaskin's seeming mistrust of the police later on in his life. Gaskin was sentenced to three years' penal servitude at Portland Prison in Dorset. It is not recorded as to whether his mother or father attended the trial.

*Chapter Nine*

# HARD LABOUR BY THE SEA

Portland Prison had been built in 1848 as the government of the day had been forced to respond to growing pressure from reform groups to improve the prison service. There was seen to be a need to provide education and training for prisoners, especially as Western Australia had made it clear that it was no longer willing to provide a penal colony for Britain's convicts.

By the time Harry Gaskin entered the gates of the prison in 1914, it had a reputation as a harsh but forward thinking environment. Gaskin's first encounter with the invigorating air of Dorset would have been at the end of a train journey, under guard from Stafford to Underhill station in Portland. He would then have been transferred up to the prison in a covered cart along with any other prisoners who were beginning their sentences at the same time.

The prisoners would then have been familiarised with the systems that operated at Portland. The daily routine would have been quickly established. A day that began early in the morning with rising followed by ablutions, breakfast and morning prayers. The convicts would then have spent around four and a half hours at labour, before returning to the prison for a hot meal around midday. The afternoon would have involved a further session of hard labour, before supper at around six in the evening. This was followed by prayers and instruction before being locked up for the night at around eight o'clock.

For Harry Gaskin this would have been a familiar routine, very similar to that he had experienced for over four years at Saltley and also probably similar to the regime he had undergone at Stafford Gaol in 1912 and also whist on remand in 1913.

The regime at Portland was strict. The warders were not encouraged to be over familiar with the convicts. Indeed, the life of the warders involved long hours, strict discipline and the threat of assault or even murder. There were perks with the job though. Warders had paid annual leave, free uniform, free medical, dental and optical treatment, along with gas, running water and free coal. The children of warders had a school to attend. The warders also enjoyed a library with function rooms, organised social events and sports facilities, confirming the forward thinking attitude of the prison service at this time.

The civilian population of Portland often worked with the convicts on a number of ongoing projects. As a result there was some tension between the two bodies of men. The free labourers felt that they worked harder than the convicts, and indeed the free labourers had to work in all weathers whereas the prisoners were marched to sheds to shelter during periods of inclement weather. The convicts received three meals a day, including a hot lunch, eaten at set times and in a dry cell, not a cold meal eaten outdoors. The Portlanders must have wondered about the effectiveness of penal servitude when they often saw prisoners return for a second or third spell at His Majesty's Pleasure! Perhaps it was the lure of heated accommodation, running water and sanitation, an unimagined luxury for the majority of law abiding citizens.

The aim of the new prison system was to offer the convicts the opportunity to train for a trade or a skill. This was not far removed from the aims of the reformatory at Saltley. Gaskin would have had plenty of choice as far as new trades were concerned. Around the prison itself there were a host of possibilities, ranging from levelling and excavation, to stone preparation, carpentry, forge and foundry work, gardening, cooking, baking and washing of laundry.

The Admiralty provided the chance of quarrying stone, masonry for the breakwater, plant and machinery repair, the supply of block stone for the Admiralty works and the crushing of stone for infill and concrete.

Not to be outdone the War Office also demanded quarrying at the Verne Citadel, masonry for the Breakwater and Nothe forts and the laying of railway systems to keep these workings supplied.

Security at the prison and its associated workings was well advanced with armed troops and armed civil guards manning lookout posts. The quarries were both arduous in terms of the work carried out and dangerous. It must be said, however, that danger was a common factor in industrial employment throughout Britain at this time. None would have known this better than Gaskin with his mining background.

This was the backdrop to the next three years of Gaskin's life. He may well have assisted in the building of the Verne Ditch at Portland. Convict labour was used in the construction of the project and the task was supervised by the Royal Engineers, a group of the Army that Gaskin was to be associated with during the Great War. This may be where this attraction was first formed.

Gaskin certainly had plenty of time to think about his mistakes and to take stock of his life. He was now in his twenty third year. His wife, son and family were a long way away in Cannock and Hednesford. It would seem that his wife left the apartment and went back to live at her parents house in Brindley Heath. Her motherly instincts may not have been fully developed for the young Arthur Henry was being brought up by Gaskin's mother at Bridgtown. This was probably due to the fact that Lizzie Gaskin had no visible means of support and was unable to care for her child. The Gaskins may well have thought that they had a natural obligation to offer help to their daughter in law; after all, the baby was the first born of their only son and was their grandchild.

*Where the body was found.*

*Five foot wall over which the body was taken.*
*The tank is several yards from the wall.*

*Funeral of the victim, March 2nd 1919.*

*Gaskin entering a taxi after the inquest at Cannock.*

*Where the victim was last seen alive.*

*Houses in St John's Road, Cannock, typical of those where the Gaskin family would have lived.*

*Miner's cottages in Huntington*
*– the Gaskin's lived in Huntington for a number of years.*

*Copy of Marriage Certificate of Henry Gaskin and Elizabeth Talbot.*

**FC** 463120

CERTIFIED COPY of an ENTRY
Pursuant to the Births and Deaths Registration Act 1953

| | | Registration District | | Lichfield | | | | | |
|---|---|---|---|---|---|---|---|---|---|
| 1894. | | **Birth in the Sub-district of** Rugeley | | | | in the County of Stafford | | | |
| Columns:- | 1 | 2 | 3 | 4 | 5 | 6 | 7 | 8 | 9 | 10 |
| No. | When and where born | Name, if any | Sex | Name, and surname of father | Name, surname and maiden surname of mother | Occupation of father | Signature, description, and residence of informant | When registered | Signature of registrar | Name entered after registration |
| 367 | Fifteenth August 1894 Brindley Heath Rugeley R S D | Elizabeth | Girl | Henry Charles Talbot | Emily Ann Talbot formerly Bailey | Coal Miner | X The Mark of Emily Ann Talbot Mother Brindley Heath Rugeley | Twenty fourth September 1894 | John Hackett Registrar | |

Certified to be a true copy of an entry in a register in my custody.

*Janet Wain Deputy* Superintendent Registrar
6th April 2005 Date

CAUTION: THERE ARE OFFENCES RELATING TO FALSIFYING OR ALTERING A CERTIFICATE AND USING OR POSSESSING A FALSE CERTIFICATE. ©CROWN COPYRIGHT
WARNING: A CERTIFICATE IS NOT EVIDENCE OF IDENTITY.

*Copy of Elizabeth Talbot's Birth Certificate.*

**FC** 699238

CERTIFIED COPY of an ENTRY
Pursuant to the Births and Deaths Registration Act 1953

| | | Registration District | | Lichfield | | | | | |
|---|---|---|---|---|---|---|---|---|---|
| 1891. | | **Birth in the Sub-district of** Lichfield | | | | in the County of Stafford | | | |
| Columns:- | 1 | 2 | 3 | 4 | 5 | 6 | 7 | 8 | 9 | 10 |
| No. | When and where born | Name, if any | Sex | Name, and surname of father | Name, surname and maiden surname of mother | Occupation of father | Signature, description, and residence of informant | When registered | Signature of registrar | Name entered after registration |
| 142 | Twenty second July 1891 Stowe Street Saint Chad Lichfield U S D | Thomas Henry | Boy | Henry Joseph Albert GASKIN | Harriet Eliza GASKIN formerly POOLE | Stone Mason Journeyman | H E Gaskin Mother Stowe Street Saint Chad Lichfield | Twenty sixth August 1891 | John Bird Registrar | |

Certified to be a true copy of an entry in a register in my custody.

*S. Bridger Deputy* Superintendent Registrar
29 October 2004 Date

CAUTION: THERE ARE OFFENCES RELATING TO FALSIFYING OR ALTERING A CERTIFICATE AND USING OR POSSESSING A FALSE CERTIFICATE. ©CROWN COPYRIGHT
WARNING: A CERTIFICATE IS NOT EVIDENCE OF IDENTITY.

*Copy of Gaskin's Birth Certificate.*

V

CRIMINAL APPEAL ACT, 1907.

R. v. _Henry Thomas Gaskin_

# LIST OF EXHIBITS.

| Number or other identifying mark on Exhibit. | Short description of Exhibit. | Produced by Prosecution or Defence. | Directions of the Judge of the Court of Trial, with name and address of person retaining Exhibit. |
|---|---|---|---|
| A | Plan | Prosecution | Clerk of Assize |
| B | Note | " | do |
| C | Envelope | " | do |
| D. | Letter | " | do |
| E | Doctor's notes | " | do |
| F | Statement of prisoner | " | do |
| No 1 | Knife. | " | Supt John Morrey Cannock |
| No 2 | Lamp book | " | do |
| No 9 | Stick | " | do |

Signed (a) _W. Ellis Gardner_
_Clerk to Committing Justices_

(a) Coroner, Clerk to Committing Justice, or Officer of Court of Trial.
Form XXXIII. Shaw & Sons, Fetter-Lane, E.C. (S85050)

_The exhibits at his trial._

*A copy of the note sent to Elizabeth Gaskin by her husband.*

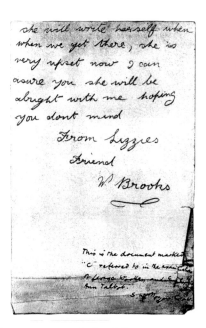

*The note dictated by Gaskin to a crippled soldier.*

*The envelope the note was delivered in.*

"F"

Feb 23rd 1919.

I, Henry Thomas Gaskin, being of a sober and sound state of mind. do make this statement of my own free will without any fear or favour.

On Wednesday the 19th of Feb. 1919. I met my wife by arrangement on the Rugeley Road about 2.30 p.m. and proceeded with her on the outscirts of the wood by the Cannock and Rugeley Collerie offices, - she said? "Why dont you come down home, theres nobody there only mother & dad." I said "come in the wood and we'll talk things over. - in the wood.- I said " What do you mean by having these bastard kids while I was away, I know you went to Yorkshire with Sgt Walker. then to Birmingham and then to London." she said " It is your fault you should have come to me instead of going to the Army." I said "Who's is this last kid you've had." She said "Its Monties he is at home now if you want to see him". I said " Ishould very much like to see him but I'm not going down Brindley Heath again. She said " Well come down home with me. I'm sure there will be no bother." I said " No never." she said "Do come home with me. I'll go to bed with you at once and you can have what you want." I said "I no use you wanting me to go there, as I never shall." she said.. "Well if you dont intend to do something to keep me I shall go back to Monty he promised to keep me if you wouldnt. but do come home with me" she starts to cry. and puts her right arm round my neck. I put my left arm round her neck. and grips her throat with my right hand. and says " You dare to ask me to go to bed with you, after what you've done. You dare to tell me you'll go back to Harris", - she struggles out of my grip and attempts to scream. I take fresh hold. and say "You're a she-devil of the first warter, and I'll send you to hell where you belong. You have had your pleasure while I was in France now I'll tare you inside out", she falls down. And I draged her some yards farther into the wood, then stood over her for

Gaskin's handwritten confession.

IX

about a minute, when she attempted to get up. I pushed her down again and said "I have not done with you yet." and hit her with my fist in the left ear, saying "thats for Sgt Walkie", hiting her in the right ear saying "Thats for your Monty, struck her in right eye. "Thats for whoring in Birmingham, struck her in left eye "Thats for whoring in London". " I then rolled my right sleeve up saying "Now I'll tare your inside out and show it you" and I forced my arm in her woumb. up to my ello, failing to draw anything out, I made about four snowballs and forced them in her inside. saying. "These should cool you down a bit." in a fainting condition she began to kick, and make a noise with her throat. . I said "I stop that now for you", and breaking a thick twig off a tree I forced it down her throat. saying "Chew that if you like. I then took my knife and cut all her clothing off and while I was hiding her hat and shoes she got into a kneeling up possition, when I got back to her she murmered "Harry" and raised her arms up lerel with her sholders. I knelt down in front of her and said " Do you see me" she shook her head, meaning no. "I said do hear me". and she nodded. "I said listen to me" I going to kill you and cut you to pieces". I kicked her under the chin and she rolled over. . I said "now we'll see what you're made of." and I cut her open from woumb to nable. I caught her by the heels and bent her up. saying "do you see that." she did not speak but put her hands over where I had cut her. I got up and put my heel on her neck until she had finished strugling. then I cut her up to the neck and pulled her bowels out. saying "Now the devil in hell can have you if he wants you, I dont. " she was still breathing when I covered her up with her own clothes saying " If you get over that well say the devil dont want you." I left her where she lay time being about 4.30 p.m. reached home about 5.30 p.m. went to cinema Walsall Rd with my brother after being in there about half an hour I made an excuse to leave the building and proceeded to Hednesford by bus. went to the wood where the body lay. draged it to the edge of the wood. cut the head.

Gaskin's handwritten confession.

off. and almost cut the left leg off. then I dragged the body to a sewer culvert near by. and took the head and clothes to the Hednesford Gasometer. reach home about 11.15 p.m. On Thursday afternoon I went to work and was met on the pit top by two of the Hednesford Police who asked me if I knew where my wife had gone. as she had not returned home since going out to meet me. after I left them I went over the common towards home. but at the corner on the Belt Rd I turned towards Hightown till I got opposite 3° pit turned on to the railway and walked along the line through Hednesford Station then turned towards the Mines Rescue Station over the common to the place where I left the body. draged it out and carried it to the Gasometer where I took the head. and forcing a two inch gas pipe down inside the ins. I lowered into the water remarking "Now you can go to Monty if you like" I left the place. reach home about 2.30 am.

I swear this statement is true

Signed  Henry Thomas Gaskin.
23 Febuary 1919.

Witness.
J.Morrey.
Actg Supt
23ʳᵈ Feby 1919

This is the document marked "B" referred to in the examination of John Morrey.
S.W.Morgan. Coroner.

*Gaskin's handwritten confession.*

XI

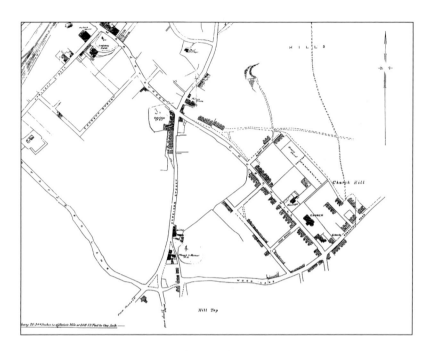

*Hednesford 1919.*

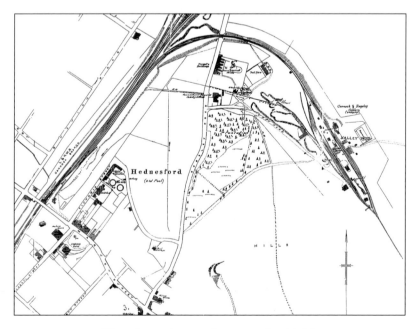

*The plantation and gas works 1919.*

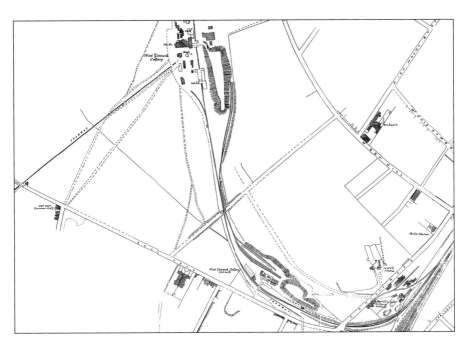

*West Cannock Colliery Pits 1 and 3.*

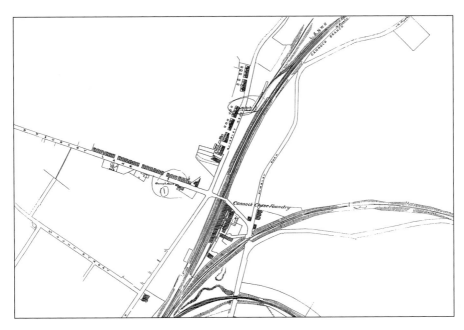

*The Talbot's house, 72 Brindley Heath.*

# SHOCKING TRAGEDY AT HEDNESFORD.

**MUTILATED BODY OF WOMAN FOUND AT THE GAS WORKS.**

**ARREST OF THE HUSBAND. THE INQUEST OPENED.**

Rumours were circulated freely during th latter end of last week that a woman was missing from Brindley Heath, and foul play was suspected. Little was known about the matter until Friday evening, when it was reported that Thomas Henry Gaskin, of Longford Lane, Bridgtown, had been arrested. Gaskin is the husband of the woman, and the suspicion of the police was aroused by a letter which the woman received from him. A strenuous search was made in the vicinity of the Hednesford Hills, and the Valley Pit, which was of no avail, and the terribly mutilated and headless remains of the deceased Elizabeth Gaskin, were found on Sunday afternoon, in the tank of the gasometer at Hednesford. Particulars of the tragedy will be found below. The accused husband did not appear to realise his position and assumed a callous demeanour. He was after the inquest, and second hearing, at a Court of Justice, conveyed to Winson Green, to await the adjourned inquest. The police are still making enquiries and it is stated that the evidence will be of a most sensational character.

THOMAS HENRY GASKIN.

THE STORY OF THE TRAGEDY.

Elizabeth Gaskin, the murdered woman was one of a family of fifteen, and daughter of Mr and Mrs Henry Charles Talbot, of Brindley Heath, Hednesford. She was 23 years of age, and with the exception of a short period of domestic service, she had lived at home. There were three brothers, one of whom was killed during the war. Six years ago she met Thomas Henry Gaskin, and they were married at Cannock Church.

Thomas Henry Gaskin, is the son of the late Mr Gaskin, and Mrs Gaskin, of Cannock. The father died about two years ago and his mother married Mr Williams, and they now reside at Longford Lane, Bridgtown. As a youth he was an enthusiastic member of the local Boy Scouts, and as a drummer he was very clever, the manner in which he manipulated the drumsticks as he lead the band, being a feature. As he grew up he appeared to become more erratic, and figured in various escapades, leading one to think that he had read some of the novelettes of a very sensational character. Eventually he joined the Army and as a disciplined soldier he, it is stated rose to the rank of Sergeant. On his demobilisation he returned to his home and commenced work at the West Cannock Colliery, where his fine physique stood him in good stead, and he was considered a good workman. His wife had left him and was still living with her parents at Brindley Heath, while he lived at Longford Lane. It appears that they had met on one or two occasions, and on Wednesday previous to the tragedy a letter was received by the deceased woman, asking her to meet him on Wednesday afternoon round the Pool, which is situate on the Rugeley Road. The deceased woman exhibited a certain amount of excitement, on the receipt of the note, and suggested to her mother that her husband desired a reconciliation. She hastily discarded the apron she was wearing in pursuing her domestic duties and catching hold of her sister's coat prepared to keep the appointment, although the mother expressed her doubts as to the sincerity of her husband, in whom she had little faith. The woman left the house proceeding in good spirits in the direction of the Pool.

THE MEETING.

It was soon after two o'clock on Wednesday afternoon, when few people would be observed on the Rugeley Road, a man and a woman were observed near the Plantation, Little notice was taken of them although it was observed by a passer by that they were apparently engaged in a wrangle. Eventually one entered the plantation from the road and the other proceeded along the road leading to the Valley Pits, and it is assumed entered the plantation from that direction. Nothing further was thought of the affair, until late at night when the deceased woman failed to return home, and the mother became anxious. The police were communicated with, and Inspector Woolley immediately organised a search party and Superintendent Morrey, of Cannock, was also communicated with, and enquiries in various directions were instituted.

THE SEARCH.

It seemed that the Plantation had a fascination for the searchers. It is a comparatively young plantation, but the trees have grown very thick, and some of them are fine specimens of firs, and pines. Try as they could, however, no trace of a tragedy is reported to have been discovered and attention was then directed to the reservoir at the colliery which is in close proximity and a thorough search was made with the drags. This proved of no avail, and attention was then directed to a culvert, but that also was drawn a blank. On Friday and Saturday a large contingent of police in mufti were drafted to Hednesford, and a thorough seach of the Hills was instigated, the constables proceeding in close and open formation as was thought desirable.

THE ARREST.

On Friday afternoon Superintendent Morrey and Inspector Woolley proceeded to the West Cannock Colliery, and met Henry Thomas Gaskin, as he left work at the pit, and he was taken to the Police Station, where he was asked relative to the disappearance of his wife. The replies not bing satisfactory to the police he was detained.

BEFORE THE MAGISTRATE.

Various rumours were now in circulation, and there was some consternation when the accused was brought from Hednesford to Cannock, in charge of Chief Superintendent Pilliner, Supt. Morrey, and Inspector Woolley, and other officers. Mr T. Mason was the justice, and the proceedings took place in the Magistrate's Clerk's Office.

The accused was charged with the suspected murder of his wife, Elizabeth Gaskin.

Gaskin exhibited a demeanour of indifference, and appeared to treat the matter lightly. The Acting Magistrates Clerk (Mr E. A. Orton) gave the usual warning, and advised him not to say anything at that stage, although he could do so if he chose.

The accused made no reply.

Inspector Woolley stated that at 4 p.m. on Friday, the 21st, in company with Supt. Morrey, he saw the accused at the West Cannock Colliery, Hednesford. The Superintendent told him that his wife could not be found and asked him to accompany him to the Hednesford Police Station. He cautioned him, and charged him on suspicion of causing his wife's death, at Hednesford, on Wednesday, February 19th. His reply was "All I can say is I didn't see her on Wednesday. That's all I have got to say."

Chief Supt. Pilliner asked for a remand in custody until Tuesday, and this was granted.

THE SEARCH CONTINUED.

In the meantime the search was being continued by the police, until the afternoon of Sunday, when a taxi was observed to stop at the Plantation. Tre occupants were police officers and the accused man Gaskin. Some little time was spent in the Plantation and eventually they emerged and again entering the taxi they proceeded in the direction of the Hednsford Old Gas Works.

It is well known that for some years gas has not been manufactured at Hednesford, but the two holders are supplied from Cannock Gas Works. Hence there is not the usual activity that was associated with the surroundings in years gone by, and the paths &c. are now grass grown. This includes the sides of the tanks which surround the gas holders.

A GRUESOME DISCOVERY.

Gaskin was taken to the Police Station and the police at once commenced dragging operations in the tank of one of the gas holders. The drags had not long been in use before some of the clothing of a woman was recovered. Soon afterwards the drags appeared to have caught hold of something, but this effort was not successful. A few minutes before five o'clock the mutilated remains of the woman were brought to the bank. The spectacle to those who witnessed it was one that will not be forgotten. The body was minus the head, and a piece of iron gas piping had evidently been pushed down the neck, and one end was protruding through the side of the body, and one of the legs was almost amputated. There were also other shocking mutilations. The remains were covered until the arrival of Dr J. K. Butter, Police Surgeon, who at once ordered their removal to the Mortuary, which was only a few yards away, and separted from the Gas Works by a wall. The search was continued for the missing head. All day Monday the drags were used without avail, and it was feared that the head had got under the gas holder. The whole of the gas was allowed to be used, and the holder was down as low as it could go. The question of emptying the water was then considered and this was understood to entail the removal of thousands of gallons. Eventually it was decided that the gas holder should be filled again, and on Tuesday morning this allowed the drags to be used more freely, and P.C. Baker first of all received an old saucepan which for some time had been resting on the bank grass by the side of the gasometer, and which the caretaker had not missed until the search was commenced on Sunday afternoon. Evenually the drags caught the hair of the head, of the woman and it was brought to the surface and taken to the mortuary at Cannock, where the body had been removed to on Sunday night.

The peculiar feature of the affair is that the width of the water between the brickwork and the gas holder is only about ten inches, and it can be readily imagined that the woman was very diminutive, and even then it would be very difficult to dispose of the body in such close quarters. The woman was very short, it is stated, under five feet in height.

OPENING OF THE INQUEST.

At 3.15 on Tuesday, Mr S. W. Morgan, (Coroner), opened the inquest in the Council Chambes, at Cannock, when nine jurymen were sworn. The Jurymen were Mr E. Lindop (foreman), Messrs S. Watkiss, T. Stephenson, John F. Stokes, F. Williams, G. M. Whitehouse, E. Birch, W. Guy and A. L. Bird. There were also present Dr J. K. Butter, Chief Supt. Pilliner, Supt. Morrey, Inspector Woolley, and the accused.

The Coroner having sworn in the jury, the remains was viewed.

The Coroner said the police report of the death was as follows :— Elizabeth Gaskin, aged 23. About 1.40 p.m. on Wednesday, the 19th of February, Emily Ann Talbot, of 72 Brindley Heath, Hednesford, mother of deceased, received a note which had been sent by Henry Thomas Gaskin, husband of the deceased. The note was as follows :—

Meet me round the pool at once—important.

The note was shown to deceased, who at once left her home to go and meet her husband. They were seen together in the vicinity of the Cannock and Rugley Colliery Offices situated in Rugeley-road, Hednesford, where there is a plantation. Deceased was not seen again until her headless and mutilated body was recovered from the water surrounding the gasometer of Hednesford Gasworks, at 4.30 p.m. on Sunday, February 23rd, by Superintendent Morrey. The deceased's head had been severed from the body, which is in a badly mutilated condition, having been cut open and an attempt made to sever the legs.

The Coroner added : When this report was sent the head had not been recovered, but I understand it was found this morning.

Emily Ann Talbot, wife of Henry Charles Talbot, miner, 72, Brindley Heath, Hednesford, identified the body as that of her late daughter, Elizabeth Gaskin, the wife of Henry Thomas Gaskin. Deceased resided at home with witness. She was 23 years of age.

At this stage the Coroner intimated he proposed to adjourn the inquiry. He had only intended taking evidence of identification. Moreover, the police had not completed their inquiries. There were many matters which they wished to investigate.

The inquiry was then adjourned until Wednesday, March 5th, at 2 p.m.

Outside the Council House a large crowd assembled with the object of securing a glance at the accused. He was immediately driven to the Police Station, and again brought before Mr T. Mason who granted a further remand, similar evidence having been submitted as at the previous Court.

# MUTILATION MYSTERY.

## WOMAN'S HEADLESS BODY FOUND IN WATER TANK.

### HUSBAND CHARGED WITH COMMITTING ATROCIOUS CRIME.

Following upon the mysterious disappearance of a young married woman, of 23, her mutilated and headless body was found in the water-tank of a gas holder at the gas works, Hednesford, Staffs. The woman's head, which was missing, had been cut off, apparently with a knife, one of the legs was almost severed, and one arm was broken at the elbow. The entire length of the front of the body was cut open, and a piece of one-inch gas piping had been thrust right through the body. The murdered woman, Mrs. Elizabeth Gaskin, who had been living with her mother at Brindley Heath, Hednesford, failed to return home on Feb. 19. The mystery of her disappearance attracted considerable attention in the district, and for a time all the efforts of the police to trace her proved absolutely futile. It was learned, however, that her husband, Henry Thomas Gaskin, 27, a miner and ex-soldier, until two months ago in the Royal Engineers, had, since his demobilisation, been living at Bridgetown, Cannock. It also transpired that he had made an arrangement to meet deceased on the afternoon she disappeared, and was seen talking to her. Subsequently, though up to then the woman's body had not been found, the husband was placed under arrest, and charged on suspicion with having murdered her, and was remanded in custody. "I did not see her on Wednesday" (the day of her disappearance) he said. "That is all I have to say." Later a number of police officers in company with Gaskin motored over to the spot near the Cannock and Rugeley Colliery, where he was alleged to have last seen his wife. After a visit to a plantation adjacent to the road the party went to Old Hednesford Pool, where

**SOME CLOTHING WAS RECOVERED**

which was recognised as that belonging to the missing woman. Later the headless body itself was recovered from about 15 feet of water which surrounds the gasometer used for supplying gas to the district. The depth of the water varies according to the quantity of gas in the tank. The body was in a shockingly mutilated state, and, as stated, had been pierced with a long length of gas tubing. It was evident that the woman had been brutally done to death and then thrust into the water. A further search for the head of the body proved ineffective for some time, but the police had good reason for supposing that that also had been flung into the water, and continued dragging operations. These were successful, and the missing part of the body was recovered. As a result of the sensational affair, the little mining town of Cannock was in a flutter of excitement, groups standing about throughout the day in the vicinity of the police station and of the building where the inquest was to be held, in the hope of catching a glimpse of accused.—The inquiry was opened by Mr. S. W. Morgan, coroner for the district. Deceased's husband, in charge of a couple of police sergeants, was in attendance. He is only 27, of fair complexion, with a bushy moustache, and normally the expression of his face might convey the idea of a genial and pleasant individual, but during the proceedings his appearance was one of dogged determination, although he roused himself at times to crack a joke

**Henry Thomas Gaskin.**

with his custodians, when his features lit up with an expansive smile.—The coroner at the outset read the report of the police on the case, which was as under:—

About 1.50 p.m. on February 19, Emily Ann Talbot, of Brindley Heath, Hednesford, mother of deceased, received a note sent by Henry Thomas Gaskin, and the note was as follows:—

"Meet me round the pool at once. Important."

The note was shown to deceased, who at once left her home to go and meet her husband. They were seen together in the vicinity of Cannock and Rugeley Colliery offices, situated in Rugeley-road, Hednesford, where there is a plantation. Deceased was not seen again until her headless and mutilated body was recovered from the water surrounding the gasometer at Hednesford Gas Works at 4.50 p.m. on February 23, by Acting Superintendent Murray. Deceased's head had been severed from the body, which is in a badly mutilated condition, having been cut open, and an attempt made to sever the legs.

—The Coroner called deceased's mother for the purpose of the identification of the body. He then intimated that there were a good many matters which the police wished to investigate, and the inquest would have to be adjourned.—Later in the afternoon accused was again brought up at the police court on a charge of murder, and was formally remanded until March 5.—Both the victim of the tragedy and her husband are well known in the district. Accused, who has always been of an adventurous turn of mind, has seen service at the front with the Royal Engineers. He returned to his old calling as a miner a couple of months ago, being employed at

*Left: The case reported in Cannock Chase Chronicle, 1919.*
*Right: News of the World, March 1919.*

*The Uxbridge Arms, Hednesford.*

*The Plough and Harrow, Hednesford.*

*A view of Market Street, Hednesford.*

*The Anglesey Hotel, Hednesford.*

The long hot summer of 1914 wore on. Whether the events of Sarajevo on 28th June filtered through to Portland prison is not clear. The presence of the Royal Engineers, the Admiralty and the War Office may have meant that the Balkan crisis was better known and understood than elsewhere in the nation. The war between Austria-Hungary and Serbia that snowballed into a major European and soon a World War would have had an impact both inside the prison itself and upon the surrounding area.

The prison was home to a number of inmates who were young and fit and able to fight for King and Country. Whether this thought had occurred to those in Whitehall is unclear. It is certainly not known how soon such ideas began to play across the minds of those incarcerated in Portland Prison, once the declaration of war became common knowledge in August 1914. To some the thought of prisoners having their sentences shortened in order to serve in the Armed Forces would have been an uncomfortable one. Others may have felt that it was an opportunity for such people to give something back to the society they had wronged. After all, time off the original sentence due to good behaviour was an accepted prison practice. Serving in the Army or Navy was a logical progression of this policy.

Harry Gaskin was one such prisoner. When war broke out he had only served a mere six months of a three year sentence. There would have been no question of Gaskin even being considered for release at this point, even to risk life and limb in the service of the King. Therefore, Gaskin stayed put for the foreseeable future. He would have received few, if any visitors and would have been reliant for news on letters sent by his own wife, his mother and father and his friends and relatives.

One such piece of welcome news that filtered through to Gaskin was the birth of the second child of William and Phoebe Bagnall. The Bagnalls lived at 75, Brindley Heath and were friends of Abner Talbot from before his first marriage. Their first baby, Rose Hannah, had been born on 31st January 1913, at a time when Gaskin would have been ending his stretch in Stafford Gaol. The second child of the couple was born on 7th December 1914 and was baptised Olive at St. Peter's, Hednesford on 31st January 1915 by J. H. Darby.

This news may well have been overshadowed by the news that Abner and Elsie May Talbot had also celebrated a happy event. The baby was born on 23rd March 1915; a girl, baptised on 21st April as Mary Ann Talbot. This suggests a close link between Abner and his younger sister of the same name, although this may have added some confusion when the name was shouted out in the Talbot household.

Whilst this news was a welcome link to home and normality, it may have also reinforced the fact that Harry Gaskin was still in prison. That he could not enjoy the celebrations with the rest of his family, and that he and Lizzie could not add to their family even if the desire to do so was there.

The fact that many of his friends and relatives were joining up for the fight against Germany and her allies would have also had an impact on Gaskin. His youngest brother in law, Uriah, had opted to leave a safe job in the West Cannock Colliery in Hednesford to answer the call of Lord Kitchener on 3rd April 1915. He had visited the recruitment office and decided to join the South Staffordshire Regiment. Abner had also decided to give up his job in the pit, which would have been seen as a necessary job for the war effort, and joined the Royal Engineers. Francis Dando, Gaskin's brother in law, also answered the call of his country, again opting to join the South Staffordshire Regiment. Harry Gaskin would have begun to feel somewhat isolated in his cell in Portland prison. This would have been especially so when he heard, as no doubt he would have, that Uriah had been sent to Gallipoli and that Abner and Francis were both in France.

The pressure to become involved in the war was mounting on Harry Gaskin. 1915 had seen some of the heaviest fighting of the war with battles at Ypres and Loos. This meant that more men were needed to fill the shortfall of young volunteers who had paid the supreme price for their country.

Hednesford was changing rapidly. It had become a transit town for soldiers with a massive training camp being built on the outskirts of Brindley Heath on Cannock Chase. Many young men of the town were in khaki and had left to serve overseas. Lizzie Gaskin had not seen her husband in 1915 for over a year. She began, according to the evidence, to supplement her lifestyle by engaging in prostitution. In May 1915, Lizzie found herself pregnant. This would have been a disaster as far as she and her family were concerned. A married woman, whose husband had been incarcerated for over twelve months, now expecting a baby that was clearly not the child of Harry Gaskin. Lizzie had little choice but to continue with the pregnancy. On 23rd February 1916 her child was born at 15, Trent Valley Road, Lichfield. The birth was registered two days later by A. N. Buek, another occupant of the house. The baby was a girl, named Elsie May Gaskin. Lizzie returned to her family home after the birth. The child was not a robust baby, and as an afterthought, almost, was baptised at St. Peter's, Hednesford, on 10th May 1916. The story had a heartbreaking sequel for only six weeks after her baptism, Elsie May Gaskin was buried on 28th June 1916.

It was shortly before this tragic turn of events that Harry Gaskin was released from prison. An early release no doubt linked to the growing need for able bodied men for the army. Given Gaskin's unhappy experience of the Army earlier in his life, this was probably a difficult choice to make.

Whether Gaskin knew of the events unfolding at Hednesford is not known. Strangely, he chose not to return to his wife and young son, preferring instead to join the Royal Engineers as 158037 Sapper Henry Thomas Gaskin. After his basic training Gaskin was despatched to the Western Front to serve in the front line around the Belgian town of Ypres.

## Chapter Ten

# FOR KING AND COUNTRY

Joining the Royal Engineers in 1916 was probably the best move that Harry Gaskin had made in his life. The basic training that many new recruits found arduous at the start would have seemed fairly straightforward to Gaskin. He was used to hard outdoor work and thus did not have the problem of adapting from an indoor job. He was also used to the discipline associated with the British Army at this time.

Although the Royal Engineers had a specific task to perform, in the sense of providing the essential support to the infantry, the soldiers would have undergone the same basic training. Gaskin and his new colleagues would have been taught how to march; would have engaged in tasks to improve fitness; been introduced to the blood curdling experience of bayonet practice and taught to fire the standard rifle of the time, the Lee-Enfield .303. Other training would have introduced the recruits to Mills bombs and the Stokes mortar. The maintenance of the trench system would also have been taught to the troops, in preparation for embarking to France.

At the end of the process, Gaskin, like many troops would have felt confident in his abilities to face the coming ordeal. The crossing to France would have been made and Gaskin would have then arrived at a camp such as Etaples, in order to receive the toughening up that the army felt was essential before soldiers were sent to the Front Line.

Although Gaskin was serving in the same Regiment as one of his brothers in law, Abner Talbot there is nothing to suggest that the two men served together. The British Army had swollen to a massive force of over two million soldiers. Frequent movement of troops meant that their paths may have crossed at some point. Indeed, it is feasible that Gaskin may have met Uriah Talbot and Francis Dando at some time during his service.

What is pretty clear is that Harry Gaskin was a good soldier. He was disciplined, brave and organised. This showed itself in steady promotion, from sapper to sergeant by the end of his service career. Service routine clearly suited him even taking into account the danger and horror that was part and parcel of the First World War.

This danger would have been brought home in July 1916. The battle of the Somme began on 1st of that month. Despite unheralded preparation and the confidence of the British High Command under Douglas Haig, the "Big Push" failed. Almost 60,000 casualties on the first day of the battle told the grim story. What was supposed to be the crucial breakthrough that would bring an end to the stalemate of trench warfare, did not materialise. Instead, attack after futile attack only increased the carnage and casualty lists. One of these attacks involved the assault on Pozieres, where an Australian Division attempted to drive up Sausage Valley, supported by a South Midland Division, attacking Mash Valley. A secondary attack on the same day, the 27th July, involved a further and sadly, unsuccessful attempt to wrest Delville Wood from German control. This involved the 2nd Battalion of the South Staffordshire Regiment, which took heavy casualties. One of the dead was Uriah Talbot who was aged 19.

This must have been a crushing and devastating shock to all who knew him. His family were informed by way of a telegram from the War Ministry of David Lloyd George. One can only imagine the impact that such news would have when looking back after such a time has passed. His mother and father may to some extent have been half expecting such a possibility. The realisation that the war was creating unimaginable losses was slowly beginning to filter through to the British public. Nevertheless, the sad loss of their nineteen year old son would have been difficult to come to terms with. His sisters Mary Ann and Lizzie would have received the news badly, as would Fred, the youngest of the family.

In France, the news may have taken longer to reach the three men who were related to Uriah, his brother, Corporal Abner Talbot, and his two brothers in law, Private Francis Dando and Sapper Henry Gaskin. The sense of loss may well have been just as deeply felt even for hardened soldiers who had become almost immune to the daily association with death.

What would not have been known at the time was that Uriah Talbot did not have a known grave. Whether this was because there was not enough of his body left to identify is not known. It may be that after an initial quick burial, his remains were disturbed by renewed shellfire. After the war Uriah Talbot's name was one of the seventy two thousand such names that appeared on the Thiepval Memorial.

Gaskin's war along with those of his relatives and friends continued through 1916. Again Gaskin was in the position of finding out what was happening back at home from letters sent by his parents and perhaps his wife. One such letter would have probably made its way to the sector of the Western Front where Gaskin was serving in early November 1916. This letter contained bad news. His mother, Harriet would have had the difficult task of telling her only son that on the 30th October, 1916, his father, Henry Joseph Albert Gaskin had died whilst down the pit. Gaskin senior had moved from the Littleton Colliery and was now employed at the Leacroft Colliery as a boiler minder. Perhaps his change in place of job had been due to increasingly poor health. He had been under the doctor for over four months, complaining of severe abdominal pain and bouts of fainting. The problem was diagnosed as gall stones. On the last day of his life, these stones impacted, causing a blockage and resulting in a very sudden and excruciatingly painful death.

How his son received this news is not certain. It would appear that father and son had not enjoyed a particularly close relationship. However, the war may have changed the perspective of both men. Thus the news of the sudden death of his father may have had quite an impact upon Harry Gaskin. He would have felt a sense of inadequacy and frustration at not being there to offer comfort and support to his mother at this important time in her life. His father had died at the age of 53. His mother was only 44 years of age, a widow, living at 43 Longford Lane, Bridgtown and with her son in constant danger in France and simply unable to come home.

The Great War did not stop for individual personal tragedies. Gaskin would have been expected to carry on with his duties on a daily basis, as he had done since arriving on the Western Front. This meant facing the threat of death and destruction without rancour. It is to Gaskin's credit that he continued to serve his country. He would have had the prospect of his first winter in the trenches. This was a test of any man, with the biting, numbing cold as an extra difficulty to be endured. By the end of the year Harry Gaskin had been in France and Belgium for almost seven months. He had no prospect of leave; a rather hit and miss affair in the British Army at this time.

The new year of 1917 saw a decline in the morale of the Army in general. The war was now entering its third year and the failure of battles such as the Somme, was beginning to sap the desire of the soldiers to consider any prospect of imminent victory. The war of attrition that had developed meant that an air of cynicism began to permeate the thoughts of the average Tommy. Gaskin would probably not have been immune to such thoughts.

However, the New Year was only a matter of two months old when a somewhat happier event would have filtered through to Mrs. Gaskin's eldest child. On 20th February 1917, she married William Henry Williams, a forty nine year old miner. The marriage took place at the Catholic Church of the Sacred Heart and Our Lady at Cannock. Presumably her new husband was a Catholic, or it may be that Harriet Gaskin had become a Catholic in the short time following her first husband's death. The ceremony of marriage was witnessed by H. W. Junemann, the groom's son and Prudence Willett. The actual service was carried out by William Rowley O'Keeffe, the Roman Catholic priest of Cannock. The forty nine year old bachelor and the forty four year old widow both gave 43, Longford Road, Bridgtown as their address.

This news may well have come as somewhat a surprise to Harry Gaskin in the trenches of the Western Front. He may have been aware of his mother's friendship with Williams, which perhaps had developed since 1904 when Williams was summonsed for assault by Mrs. Gaskin. Yet the time scale of only three and a half months since the death of his father seems strangely short even taking into account the impact of the war on the day to day lives of the citizens of Britain. Whenever his leave was due Gaskin now had to get used to a step father.

Indeed, Harry Gaskin would have to wait until September 1917 for his first leave. By that time the battle of Passchendaele had been raging for two months. Gaskin must have felt a mixture of emotions as he made his way back to Cannock from the slaughter of the Western Front. He would no doubt have been looking forward to seeing his mother and family again after such a long parting from them. Yet he would have had the uncertainty of meeting a step father. More importantly, perhaps was the prospect of seeing his wife Lizzie for the first time since he was sent to Portland in February 1914.

In the intervening period, it would appear that Lizzie had been rather less than the dutiful wife. She had already had one illegitimate child whilst Gaskin had been in prison. Her service allowance had been stopped by the Army on account of her behaviour. Lizzie was suspected of being a prostitute. Indeed, her conduct had been investigated by Hednesford police. Hence any meeting between them was likely to be fraught. Harry Gaskin arrived at Cannock station on 28th September 1917 and went straight to his mother's house. The news of Gaskin's return did not take long to travel the three miles or so to Brindley Heath where Lizzie was living with her parents. She appeared at the Williams' house on Sunday 30th September, making, according to Mrs. Williams a terrible row on the pavement outside the house. Lizzie then came round the back of the house and continued to make a racket. Harry Gaskin said that he wanted nothing more to do with her and was in such a rage that he threatened to shoot his wife, grabbing his service rifle. Only the timely intervention of Gaskin's mother stopped a tragedy.

This event would no doubt have provided the immediate neighbours with entertainment at the time although the serious nature of the scene would not have been lost on the more perceptive of them. Had Gaskin pulled the trigger, then he would have been on a murder charge whilst a serving soldier. It is a moot point, but he may well have received a more sympathetic hearing had this been the outcome in 1917. The incident would have also been a real eye opener to his new step father and step brother.

What is absolutely stunning is that by the end of his week's leave Gaskin and his wife would appear to have forgotten the incident. He went to her mother's house in Brindley Heath where the couple apparently lived together as man and wife for the first time since 1914. This would suggest that there existed some kind of affection, if not deep seated love between them.

Yet when Henry Gaskin returned to France on 7th October 1917 a number of thoughts and emotions would have returned with him. The beginning of his leave had been every bit as bad as he had feared. He had lost his temper completely and had come to within a whisper of shooting his wife. Yet by the end of the week they had seemingly made up with each other. They had lived together with Lizzie's parents whilst having their meals with

Gaskin's family at Bridgtown. Deep down, however, nagging away inside him was the fact that his wife had been a prostitute and that once he was back in France she might well return to this lifestyle. Gaskin was a proud man and was aware that he and his wife were now the likely topic of conversation in many of the pubs in Cannock and Hednesford. Such an introverted man would have found this state of affairs very uncomfortable indeed.

The war continued and so did Gaskin's contribution to the proceedings. He had decided to join a Tunnelling Company. This was a volunteer branch of the Royal Engineers, consisting of men who, usually, had a coal mining background. The task this group of men was given was to mine under the German trenches in order to lay explosives. This had been used to good effect at Messines Ridge and at the commencement of the battle of Passchendaele. The tunnellers were well paid, quite probably an important factor for Gaskin. The work was not without its dangers though. There were not only the usual risks associated with mining underground, such as the tunnel collapsing, but the very real chance of the tunnel being deliberately collapsed by German counter mining. This is precisely what happened at some point in 1918. As a result of a German explosion under a tunnel being dug by the Tunnelling Company Gaskin belonged to, he was buried alive. This must have been a terrifying ordeal for all concerned. Yet men deal with trauma differently, depending on the state of their nerves and general mental strength. So for Gaskin this was a shattering experience. He was out of the line for about four days whilst he recovered sufficiently to be able to resume his duties. He carried on with his tasks seemingly none the worse physically at least, for his encounter. Mentally was a completely different question. After the incident, Harry Gaskin began to act strangely. There were reports that he started to shoot at empty bottles in No Man's Land; that he began to take unnecessary risks which were out of character. Gaskin also ventured into Ypres whilst it was under heavy shellfire and wandered around apparently oblivious to the danger that he faced. To some people it was as if Sapper Henry Thomas Gaskin no longer cared about his life.

As the war approached its end, Gaskin came home on leave for the second time in October 1918. If he was expecting to see his wife then he was to be disappointed. Lizzie had gone to London with another soldier and it would appear was once more engaged in prostitution. Gaskin must have written to her about his leave for whilst he was at home with his mother, a letter arrived. The letter was signed Lily Fern but Mrs. Williams recognised the handwriting as being that of Lizzie Gaskin. Lizzie asked Harry to meet her at Euston Station on his way back to the Front. Mrs. Williams may well have been fearful of her son's reaction after his first leave and so decided not to show the correspondence to her son. Instead she cut off the address and sent it on to Harry when he had returned to France. The rest of the leave passed uneventfully. Mrs Williams noticed that her son was smoking more than he had previously and that his hand tremor was worsening. This tremor may have been simply a benign one brought on by problems with close control movements. It could, of course, have been the onset of Parkinson's disease. Perhaps it was merely a reaction to the tremendous strain, both physical and mental that her son was undergoing at the time. Whatever the reason this tremor would have been a worry to any mother. On 2nd November 1918, Harry Gaskin returned to the Western Front.

A mere nine days later, the fighting in the First World War came to an end, following the signing of an Armistice. The thoughts of the Army and those of the soldiers turned to what would happen in the future. No doubt there were many people in Britain with similar concerns. As for Harry Gaskin, he was in one of the first waves of young men to be returned to civilian life. His demobilisation came into effect on the 4th January 1919 and he returned to his mother's house two days later, on the very day that his wife was giving birth to a son at 72, Brindley Heath. Gaskin went off to Ripon to be officially discharged from the Army, returning to Bridgtown towards the end of the month. One of his first acts on return was to contact Mr. Tench, a solicitor at Wednesbury about the possibility of a divorce from his errant wife, Elizabeth.

## Chapter Eleven

# MURDER

The Great War had not exactly been kind to the Talbot family. The loss of Uriah in July 1916 came on top of the birth and death of Lizzie's illegitimate daughter, Elsie May, between February and June of the same year. There were also investigations into the conduct of Lizzie who, it would seem, had become a common prostitute, taking advantage of the setting up of an Army Training camp just outside Brindley Heath.

In 1917, the situation between Lizzie and Harry Gaskin had worsened on Harry's first leave, although this had been patched up by the end of his furlough. However, by October 1918, when Harry came home on leave for a second time, his wife was in London, apparently earning an immoral living.

If this was not bad enough for the family to assimilate, on 1st December 1918 the funeral took place at St. Peter's of Elsie May Talbot, the second wife of Abner who was still serving in the Royal Engineers. This must have been a savage blow for the Talbot family to bear, just as the good news of the end of the war was beginning to give renewed hope to the country as a whole. By one of those strange coincidences, she too died of pneumonia, aged 25. Abner, or Bill as he was more usually known, was present at the death of his wife.

Just a month later, Lizzie Gaskin gave birth to a second son, on 6th January 1919. The father certainly was not Harry Gaskin, but was believed to be a soldier from the camp named Monty Harris. The name chosen by the mother was Uriah. A baptism took place on 30th January at St. Peter's, Hednesford.

This was the backdrop to Harry Gaskin's return from France. After securing his demobilisation, Gaskin then tried to find work. He was successful and managed to be re-engaged at his old pit, West Cannock Number Three. He was taken on as a miner, presumably on the strength of his wartime service record. Gaskin was annoyed by a couple of visitations from his wife, one of which took place at the pit head. It would appear that Lizzie wanted the couple to try and repair their marriage. Gaskin was determined to end the sorry affair and was adamant that he would proceed with divorce proceedings. He made it very clear that he did not welcome these attempts by his wife to see him. Gaskin simply wanted to get on with his life.

His life was troubled, however. He was the subject of gossip and Gaskin was fast becoming the laughing stock of the area. After all, his wife was going around with another man with whom she had had a second child in three years. Perhaps the fact that Lizzie wanted to carry on with the marriage was a concept beyond the understanding of Harry Gaskin.

On Wednesday 19th February, Gaskin got up at his mother's house in Bridgtown, and played the piano for a little while before going out for some cigarettes. Gaskin was having piano lessons which may have helped calm a troubled spirit. He was smoking more than he had ever smoked before, each cigarette being accompanied with the distinctive shaking of his hand. He was next seen by Elsie May Garry at around 10:40 in the morning. Gaskin was coming up Bradbury Lane on the way towards Green Heath. They had a brief conversation, Gaskin telling her that he had come out of the Army on 1st February. This would have been of interest to Mrs. Garry as her husband, John Thomas Garry, whilst on leave, was still wearing the khaki uniform of the British Army.

Indeed, Mr. Garry and Gaskin then struck up a conversation. The two men had never seen each other before and could hardly be called friends, but they accompanied each other towards the station in Hednesford. After passing the station, the two men went into the Anglesey Hotel where they each consumed three pints of beer. Whilst they were in the Anglesey, Gaskin passed a folded note to Tom Saunders. Saunders lived at Brindley Heath or Tackeroo as it was known colloquially. He was asked to pass the note to Mrs. Talbot at 72, Brindley Heath. Meanwhile Garry and Gaskin continued their new found friendship and pub crawl, next visiting the Uxbridge Arms. Here a further two or three glasses of rum were drunk by each man and a couple of pints of beer. Certainly Tom Saunders thought that Gaskin had had more than enough drink for a morning, although Garry felt that Gaskin was none the worse for the volume of alcohol he had downed. Gaskin and Garry left the Uxbridge at around one o' clock and made their way up the hill to the Plough and Harrow. Here a further pint of beer was consumed by each man. The two then parted company. Garry went off down Stafford Lane and Gaskin made his way towards Hednesford. Gaskin had told Garry that he had an appointment before the two of them went into the Anglesey Hotel. He did not tell Garry with whom the appointment had been made.

Tom Saunders did as he had been asked and delivered the note to Mrs Talbot at 72, Brindley Heath. Mrs Talbot was illiterate and so the note was given to her younger daughter, Mary Ann, to read. The note said "Meet me round the pool at once important". The handwriting was that of Harry Gaskin and Lizzie Talbot, on hearing this, began to get excited, feeling that her husband wanted to discuss getting back together again. Her mother tried to dissuade her daughter from responding to the note, but Lizzie was determined. She grabbed her sister's overcoat and made her way out of the house into the cold February afternoon. The pool, now the site of Hednesford Park, was around fifteen minutes walk from the Talbots' house and so Lizzie would have probably arrived at around two o'clock.

At that time Harry Gaskin was just coming out of the Plough and Harrow and so he would not have arrived to keep his appointment until around two fifteen. Lizzie and Harry were next seen by Norah Degwell who lived at 10, Rugeley Road, Hednesford. She saw them walking along the Rugeley Road obviously quarrelling at around 2:30 to 2:45 in the afternoon. Perhaps Lizzie had been annoyed at being kept waiting, especially as her husband had turned up considerably the worse for drink, something that Gaskin was not in the habit of doing. Lizzie was wearing a dark mackintosh over a pinafore and a dark blue skirt. She had on a black hat with a feather in the hat band. Gaskin was wearing a dark suit. Norah Degwell saw them go as far as the offices of the Cannock and Rugeley Colliery Company which was on the corner of the Rugeley Road and the road leading up to the Valley Pit.

Here, the couple were seen by Thomas Henry Borton who was the Chief Sales Clerk of the Colliery Company. He too noticed that the couple were arguing, particularly noting that Lizzie was talking loudly. Lizzie and Harry then stood on the corner of the plantation of trees, before Lizzie went up the path that leads to the Valley Pit whilst Harry went on around 150 yards before he too turned into the plantation. It was at this point that Thomas Henry Borton lost sight of Harry and Lizzie Gaskin.

For what happened next, we are totally reliant on the statement that Harry Gaskin made to Cannock police four days afterwards. According to Gaskin, he and Lizzie reached the outskirts of the wood. Lizzie said to Gaskin, "Why don't you come down home, there's nobody there, only Mother and Dad". Gaskin, in reply, said, "Come in the wood and we'll talk things over". Once they had reached the wood, Gaskin's mood seemed to change. "What do you mean by having these bastard kids while I was away? I know you went to Yorkshire with Sergeant Walker, then to Birmingham and then to London". Lizzie's response was to try and blame Gaskin for the situation. "It is all your fault, you should have come to me instead of going into the Army". Gaskin then asked, "Whose is this last kid you've had?" Lizzie replied, "Its

Montie's, he is at home now if you want to see him". Gaskin retorted, "I should very much like to see him, but I'm not going down Brindley Heath again". Lizzie was now becoming desperate. She was aware that her husband had been drinking heavily and she had never seen the effect that alcohol had on Gaskin. She said, "Well come down home with me. I'm sure there will be no bother". Such a suggestion did not sit easily with Gaskin, "No, never," was his response. Lizzie then tried to use sex as a bargaining tool. "Do come home with me. I'll go to bed with you at once and you can have what you want". Again the ploy backfired on Lizzie. Gaskin said, "It's no use you wanting me to go there, as I never shall". Not only was Lizzie getting desperate, she was also becoming exasperated by a husband who was seemingly immune to her entreaties. Her next words were ill chosen and almost the last words she would speak. "Well, if you don't intend to do something to keep me I shall go back to Monty, he promised to keep me if you wouldn't, but do come home with me". At this point, Lizzie began to cry and put her arm around Gaskin's neck. If the intention was to jog Gaskin into tenderness and affection, then this move was a complete failure. Harry put his left arm around her neck and gripped her throat with his right arm. He was now on the point of losing control, such was his anger and revulsion towards his wife. "You dare to ask me to go to bed with you, after what you've done. You dare to tell me you'll go back to Harris". The words were snarled at his wife. For perhaps the first time Lizzie began to feel afraid and to panic. She struggled out of his grip and tried to scream. Gaskin took a fresh hold. "You're a she devil of the first water, and I'll send you to hell where you belong", was Gaskin's next snarled phrase. "You have had your pleasure while I was in France, now I'll tear you inside out". Lizzie fell down, whether in a faint is not clear. Gaskin stood over her for about a minute, perhaps considering what he would do next. Lizzie began to struggle to her feet, but was roughly pushed down again by a man now almost out of control. "I have

71

not done with you yet". Gaskin then began an assault on his wife's head and face. He was a powerful man and the blows had the effect of loosening several teeth, causing severe bruising and a lot of bleeding, almost severing the left ear from the side of her head. Gaskin's reasoning for this savage battering was payment for Lizzie's conduct during the war, her whoring and affairs with two soldiers. Gaskin then rolled up his sleeve and attempted to pull out his wife's womb. As this failed he then inserted about four snowballs into her vagina. Lizzie now began to kick and made a noise with her throat. Gaskin was now too far gone to see sense and show compassion. Instead, he found a twig from a nearby tree and forced this down his wife's throat. Gaskin cut off his wife's clothing with his Army jack knife and hid her hat, shoes and stockings in the wood. When he came back to Lizzie, she had managed to struggle into a kneeling position. She murmured, "Harry" and raised her arms to her shoulders. Due to the beating she had received she could not see her husband but she could hear him. Just in case there was any doubt, Gaskin told her that, "I'm going to kill you and cut you in pieces". A vicious kick underneath her chin sent her reeling and probably rendered her almost senseless. Gaskin was as good as his word. He took his Army knife and cut her from womb to navel, then catching her by the heels and bending her double to see his handy work. Lizzie did not speak, she was probably incapable of uttering any sound; she simply and pathetically put her hands over the gaping wound. Gaskin then put his heel on the neck of the unfortunate woman and held it there until she finished struggling. His next act was to cut her up to the neck, pulling out her bowels. "Now the devil in hell can have you if he wants to, I don't". Gaskin then covered her with her own clothes, noticing that she was still breathing. "If you get over that, we'll say the devil don't want you", was Gaskin's parting shot to his dying wife. He then left her in the woods and according to his statement made his way home. The time had passed for it was now around four thirty.

Gaskin was seen on the way home by two people who knew him. The first was Joseph Owen Roadway, a miner who recognised Gaskin as they passed each other. Gaskin was on his way towards Hightown and was opposite the gate to Lee's Farm. Roadway said, "How do, Harry", receiving the customary "How do" in reply. Roadway noticed that Gaskin was wearing a dark grey suit, in all probability his demob suit. As was common at the time, Gaskin was also sporting a flat cap. Roadway noted that Gaskin was walking normally and did not seem strange in any way. Roadway set the time at four fifteen.

The next person to see Gaskin was Daisy Winfer. She lived at 41, Longford Lane, just next door to his mother's house. Daisy had been into Cannock and was waiting in Church Street to catch a bus back to Bridgtown. Daisy put the time at around four forty five. Gaskin greeted her and she acknowledged him. She noted that it blew five o' clock as the bus arrived in Bridgtown. Daisy also noted that Gaskin seemed peculiar in his eyes; something that she had noticed since his return from France. Daisy had also been aware that Gaskin appeared to prefer his own company since demobilisation.

Gaskin claimed that he arrived at home at around five thirty, a fact supported by his mother. He had his tea and then later on went out to the Picture House at Cannock with his step brother Herbert Wilfred Junemann. Wilfred, as he was usually known, had been given the job, by Mrs. Williams, of keeping Harry away from his wife, following her son's return from France. The two men managed to catch the second half of the programme, but had only been there half an hour when Gaskin made an excuse and left the cinema. Wilfred had noticed that his step brother seemed unusually excited.

Gaskin caught a bus back to Hednesford and then made his way back to the wood. He dragged his wife's body further back into the wood, to where the plantation was separated from the common by a fence. Here, Gaskin severed his wife's head from her body with his knife, the cut being made between the fifth and sixth vertebrae. He then tried but failed to cut off her leg. Gaskin was probably aware that a headless, dismembered body would be more difficult to identify. He had served on the Western Front for over two years and this fact had registered only too well. Gaskin dragged the headless corpse to a culvert near to the Valley Pit and then took the head and clothes to the unused gas works in Victoria Street. Climbing over the five foot wall he pushed the head into the water under the gasometer. Gaskin then caught the bus back to Bridgtown and arrived there at eleven fifteen, some twenty minutes after his step brother.

The following morning, it would appear that Gaskin got up as usual and had his breakfast. At around ten thirty there was a knock at the door. For Gaskin this would have no doubt made him start, especially when on opening the door he saw his mother-in-law standing there. Emily Talbot opened with "You are just the man I want to see". Harry Gaskin was taken aback and replied with a hastily gulped "Oh!" Gaskin obviously did not want the rest of the household to hear the conversation and so came out of the house, pulling the door to behind him and then walked down the entry. Mrs. Talbot then said "Harry, what did you do with Lizzie yesterday?" Gaskin tried to deny that he had seen her. Emily Talbot may not have been the brightest woman in the district, but she was not to be denied. "But you did see her. You sent the note by Tom Saunders, didn't you?" Gaskin admitted sending the note but then went on to say that he had intended to see Lizzie and tell her not to follow him as he was seeking a divorce, but had not kept the appointment. Mrs. Talbot said "Harry, it doesn't matter. She's got to be found. I am going to see the police about her". With that she left Gaskin where he was and made her way back to Hednesford police station where she reported the fact that her daughter was missing and that her daughter's husband was very much in the frame.

Gaskin must now have been beginning to panic. He did not tell anyone in the house who had been the caller at the house. Instead, he got ready for work and made his way to West Cannock Number Three Pit for the afternoon shift. He worked as normal and came off shift at around midnight. As he came up to the top of the shaft he was met by Inspector George Woolley of Hednesford police. Gaskin probably felt that the game was up, but he managed to keep things together. Woolley told him that the police were making enquiries about his missing wife. Woolley stating that he, Gaskin, and his wife had been seen by the road near the Valley Pit. She had not been seen since and the police wanted Gaskin to give any information that he could. Gaskin again denied having seen his wife, instead claiming that he had left the pub and decided to walk home, arriving in Bridgtown at around three o'clock. Gaskin said that he felt that if he had seen his wife it might jeopardise his divorce case. Woolley had began to make enquiries, however, and told Gaskin that he had been seen on a bus at Cannock at about half past four, getting off at Wootton's corner. Gaskin claimed that any such sighting was merely mistaken identity, once more saying that he had not seen his wife on that Wednesday. The Inspector was happy to leave it at that and did not charge or caution Gaskin.

Gaskin then ostensibly made his way back towards Bridgtown. As soon as he was out of sight, he doubled back. He was now very badly spooked and panic was beginning to rise its head again. The body of Elizabeth, minus its head was in a culvert on the road near the Valley Pit. It could be found at any moment, or so it seemed to Gaskin. He therefore decided to retrieve the body and take it to the same gasometer that now housed the head and clothing of his dead wife. Pulling the body out of the sewer, Gaskin looked for some form of transport for the body. His gaze fell on a wheelbarrow lying unused and inviting at the pit. He moved the wheel barrow intending to place his wife's remains in it and then take these to the watery grave. Something made Harry Gaskin think twice. Whether he was aware of miners at the pit head is not clear. The snow was still on the ground and Gaskin thought that the barrow might leave tracks which would be only too easy to trace. Instead, Gaskin picked up the headless torso and carried it the five or six hundred yards to the disused gas works, amazingly unseen. He climbed over the five foot wall and then pushed a six foot length of one inch gas pipe through the neck of the body, one end coming out near the hip. Gaskin then pushed the body into the cold murky waters to join the severed head. "Now you can go to Monty if you like". Gaskin then made his way home arriving at around two thirty in the morning.

There would be no lie in for Gaskin. He was up the next morning and then caught the train from Hednesford to Birmingham. On arriving at New Street Station, he found an old soldier who was a cripple. Gaskin offered the man half a crown if he would write a letter at Gaskin's dictation. "Mrs. Talbot, Lizzie is quite alright, she is with me now. I met her at Hednesford on Thursday. She was crying, she told me her husband was making a fool of her, so I told her to leave all and come with me. She will send you some money when we get to London, we are going there next week. She will write herself when we get there, she is very upset now. I can assure you she will be alright with me. Hoping you don't mind. From Lizzie's friend, W. Brooks".

The letter was then addressed to 72, Brindley Heath, Hednesford, Staffs, and posted in Birmingham. Gaskin then made his way back home to Bridgtown, feeling that he had covered his tracks and put together an alibi that would at the very least give him breathing space.

Gaskin's breathing space was to be very short lived for, as he made his way to the pit to begin the afternoon shift on Friday 21st February, he was met by two police officers. One was Inspector Woolley of Hednesford police, the other was Superintendent Morrey. Gaskin was told that his wife had still not been found and was invited to accompany the officers to Hednesford Police station. Here Gaskin was cautioned and then charged with the murder of his wife at Hednesford on the 19th February 1919. Gaskin's reply was consistent to his story thus far. "All I can say is

I didn't see her on Wednesday, that's all I've got to say". Gaskin was then searched and a jack knife was found on a spring hook and his lamp hook was found in his jacket pocket. Later that day at around six twenty in the evening, Inspector Woolley went to Bridgtown and removed other items of clothing from his mother's house. This may have been the first time that Mrs. Williams realised that her son had been arrested for murder.

On Saturday 22nd February 1919, Gaskin was taken to Cannock where he appeared before Mr. Thomas Mason J. P. at a Special Court, where a formal application was made by Chief Superintendent Pilliner, of Cannock Police, to keep Gaskin on remand until Tuesday 25th February. Gaskin was taken from the Court to the cells at Cannock Police Station.

*Chapter Twelve*

# BEFORE THE MAGISTRATES

T he case against Henry Thomas Gaskin for murder was gathering pace while Harry Gaskin was languishing in the cells of Cannock Police Station. The police had been conducting searches around Hednesford in an unsuccessful attempt to find the body of the missing woman. Indeed, just before Gaskin had been arrested, Woolley and Morrey had searched the wood next to the Valley Pits without finding any trace of the body, or any sign of a scuffle. The police had also been finding witnesses who had seen the couple on the day of the murder, or who had seen Gaskin at any time on that fateful Wednesday.

The breakthrough came on Sunday, 23rd February 1919. Gaskin was still in the cells at Cannock Police Station, where he had been eating well, by all accounts, even asking for leftovers. Superintendent John Morrey received a message from Gaskin, the prisoner stating that he wanted to see the police officer in his office. Sergeant Heath was also invited into the office at Gaskin's request. Gaskin then asked Morrey if they could go to Hednesford and search for the body without the Hednesford police knowing. Morrey assured Gaskin that this was not a problem. Gaskin then said, "Well I will take you and show you where it is. You will need two drags and two men to pull them in opposite directions. She is in pieces. I cut her head off and tried to cut her leg off, it is holding on with the sinews".

Morrey, with Sergeants Brough, Harrington and Heath and Gaskin then made their way to Victoria Street in Hednesford by taxi. Gaskin got out, shouted "Over here", scaled the five foot wall, and standing by the gasometer eleven yards from the wall pointed to where he had disposed of the body. Oddly, Gaskin now seemed keen to help, actually untying the rope and dropping it into the water. After a few moments, Gaskin then offered to show the police where the crime had taken place. Morrey, Brough, P. C. Bate and Gaskin piled back into the taxi for the short drive to the plantation opposite the Valley Pit. Gaskin led the way into the wood showing the police where he had butchered the unfortunate woman. Gaskin then found Lizzie's hat, stockings and shoes and even went as far as to find the stick that he had forced down the throat of his wife.

Gaskin was then driven back to Cannock and placed once more into the cells. At seven o'clock on the same evening, Gaskin asked to see Morrey for the second time that day. Morrey travelled from home, arriving at the police station at eight. In his cell Harry Gaskin informed the Superintendent that he wanted to make a written statement. Gaskin was taken to the office, warned that any such statement had to be of his own free will, and was then given paper on which to write. The statement made chilling reading and catalogued much of what had been done to poor Lizzie Gaskin. On its completion, Gaskin signed it and asked Morrey to witness it.

Meanwhile, in Hednesford, the dragging for the body had continued. Sergeant Heath felt the drag catch on something and pulled the grisly remains of Lizzie Gaskin to the surface of the water. The body was covered and Dr. Butter, the police surgeon, was sent for. He, on arrival, ordered the remains to be conveyed to Hednesford mortuary which was next to the gasworks. The body was then taken to Cannock mortuary for a post mortem examination.

This was conducted on Monday 24th February. The examination confirmed much of what Gaskin had admitted to in his statement, although it also showed acts of sexual depravity that Gaskin had not mentioned. This included cuts on the breasts and the removal of most of the vagina, which was never found, along with cuts and abrasions around the back passage of the victim. Butter also noted that Lizzie Gaskin had had pleurisy in the period shortly before her death. He was not able to confirm any contraction of sexual disease due to the absence of most of the private parts.

Still the dragging operation continued. On Tuesday, 25th February, P. C. Baker pulled out a saucepan and on the next drag felt the rope catch on something. This turned out to be the hair of the murdered woman and within a few minutes the missing head was brought to the surface. Baker had the distasteful job of placing the head in to a Gladstone bag and transporting it to the mortuary at Cannock. Dr. Butter's first job was to show the head to Mrs. Talbot who confirmed that it was that of her missing daughter. Butter then carried out a post mortem examination of the head. This showed that Gaskin's statement had been largely true when describing the assault and battery of his wife.

Still the police carried on the preparation of their case against Gaskin. Cannock Police were clearly determined to ensure that evidence was collected and assessed thoroughly.

At 3:15 in the afternoon of Tuesday 25th February, Gaskin was taken from his cell at Cannock to the Council Chamber at Cannock. This was the chosen venue for the inquest into the death of Elizabeth Gaskin. The coroner, Mr. S. W. Morgan, swore in nine jurors, the foreman of whom was Mr. Earnest Lindop. The police were represented by Chief Superintendent Pilliner, Superintendent Morrey, Inspector Woolley and Dr. J. K. Butter as police surgeon. The accused, Henry Thomas Gaskin, was also present. Morgan listened to the basic story of the murder and heard from the mother of the deceased who confirmed the identity of her daughter, whose head had only been recovered that morning. He then decided to adjourn the inquest until Wednesday 5th March at 2pm. A large crowd had gathered outside the Council Chamber with the hope of catching a glimpse of Gaskin. The police whisked the accused away in a taxi, back to the cells, from where he was then transferred to Winson Green Prison.

The period between the inquest and the formal hearing was taken up in the Talbot household by the arrangements for the funeral of Elizabeth Gaskin. This took place on Sunday 2nd March 1919. The coffin was placed on chairs outside the family home at 72, Brindley Heath. The family and mourners sang the hymn "Jesu, lover of my soul", the assembled people being given the sheets by the undertaker, verse by verse. The body was then taken by horse drawn carriage to St. Peter's Church, where the service was conducted by the Reverend W. C. Boucher. There were a tremendous number of people who, perhaps for a variety of reasons, wanted to pay their respects by filing past the grave. They were organised into a single file in order to do this by Inspector Woolley of the Hednesford Police.

Gaskin was ferried from Winson Green on 5th March by taxi, in the presence and custody of Sergeant Heath. The inquest reconvened at the appointed hour. Gaskin now had legal representation in the shape of Mr. R. A. Tench of Wednesbury. Tench was the solicitor from whom Gaskin had sought advice on divorce proceedings in January. Gaskin was reported as looking well and taking a keen interest in the proceedings. This was in sharp contrast to his demeanour at his arrest, when his almost callous indifference was commented upon.

The saga of the marriage of the Gaskins began to unfold. Yet the story was somewhat confused and littered with errors and mistakes. The date of the marriage was recorded accurately, but Gaskin joining the Army was said to be May 1917, a full year later than the reality. It was also declared that he came home on leave in February 1918, whereas this had been September 1917. Some facts were accurately noted. The letter received by Mrs. Talbot on 22nd February, bearing a Birmingham postmark, could not be disputed.

Dr. Butter's evidence was customarily concise and correct. He concluded that Elizabeth Gaskin had died, not from strangulation, but from shock, loss of blood and the extensive wounds she had received. On hearing this, Mr. Morgan commented that this death was the work of a fiend and was beyond comprehension. Gaskin was then asked if he had anything to say and replied, "No, sir". The jury returned a verdict of wilful murder and the prisoner was again remanded to appear at a formal hearing on Thursday 13th March. A poignant touch was the embrace given to her son by Mrs. Williams as she passed him in the hearing. Both the world of her son and her own world were falling around them both.

On his return to Winson Green, Gaskin was again looked after by Sergeant Heath. The normally taciturn Gaskin decided to confide in the police officer. "I have been under observation since being in prison. I thought of going potty but I didn't want the straight jacket and the padded cell". Gaskin then went on to say that he had gone to Birmingham on Friday 21st February and had dictated the letter from Brooks to someone he had met outside New Street Station. In his considered opinion, Heath felt that Gaskin was the same now as he had always been, and Heath had known him for over seven years.

The following day, at Cannock Police Station, Dr. Butter carried out an examination of articles of Gaskin's clothing, together with his lamp hook and jack knife. He was looking for traces of blood and found some on the knees of the trousers Gaskin had been wearing on the day of the murder. Butter concluded that these rather large stains had occurred when Gaskin had been in a kneeling position. Spots were also found on the flannel shirt that he tested and on the underpants. Interestingly, Gaskin had still been wearing these pants when he was arrested on the Friday. Blood was also found both on the knife and a smear on the lamp hook.

Meanwhile, Gaskin was correct in his assertion that he was being assessed for any insanity. Dr. Cassels, the Medical Officer at the prison, was taking special note of any contact or conversations that he had with Gaskin. His conclusion was that Gaskin had been sane when he committed the crime and that he had a clear recollection of his actions. The case against Harry Gaskin was becoming as water tight as the authorities could make it.

This became apparent at the formal hearing held at the Public Rooms at Cannock on Thursday 13th March. Gaskin was again transported from Winson Green Prison in a taxi, arriving at the Rooms some time before the commencement of the hearing. It was noted that Gaskin's demeanour had changed since the inquest and that he made his way from the taxi with his head held low. Gaskin was placed into the ante room next to where the hearing would take place. The magistrates were F. D. Bumstead, Thomas Mason and W. H. Gallatley, who had been aware of Gaskin's many misdeeds over a number of years. The Police case was handled by Mr. S. Pearce on behalf of the Director of Public Prosecutions. Gaskin was represented by Mr. R. A. Tench.

An interesting point was that only a few people were allowed into the public gallery and no women were admitted.

The proceedings to some extent mirrored the inquest. Mrs. Talbot gave evidence of identification and confirmed that her daughter had had two illegitimate children while Gaskin had been in the Army, although she denied that Lizzie had had children while Gaskin had been in prison between 1914 and 1916. Mrs. Talbot claimed that she had not known that her daughter was pregnant at the time of her marriage, although she stated that Lizzie had told her later that Gaskin was not the child's father. She also told the hearing that Lizzie and Harry had lived together amicably following the row on his first leave in 1917. Mrs. Talbot also confirmed that her daughter had been "walking out" with a soldier from the nearby camp who was the father of the child born in January of 1919. Mrs. Talbot also said that her daughter's Army allowance had been stopped and that she had worked in service after this money had ceased.

The fact that the police had been diligently discovering evidence now became apparent. Tom Saunders confirmed the delivery of the note to the Talbot household, although he could not say definitely that the note shown was the same one he had taken. Norah Degwell said she now recognised the man that she had seen on the 19th with Mrs. Gaskin as the prisoner. This was offset by Sarah Southall's evidence and that of Mr. Borton, neither of whom were willing to say that the man they had both seen at different times on the 19th was Gaskin. Joseph Roadway was not able to confirm that Gaskin was intoxicated when he saw him after the murder had been committed.

The eccentricity of Gaskin's behaviour was confirmed by the police officers who said that whilst he had acted strangely at times in his life, there was nothing to suggest that he was in any way insane. This was confirmed by Dr. Butter who had known Gaskin all his life and had examined him when he was a boy and just before he was sent to Saltley Reformatory in 1906.

At this point the hearing was adjourned to be reconvened the following day in the morning. Sergeant Heath told of his conversation with Gaskin on the 5th March and Harrington and Baker told of the finding of the body and head of the deceased. The police evidence also confirmed that Lizzie Gaskin had not lived a good life and that her Army allowance had been stopped because of her immoral behaviour.

When Mr. Tench rose to conduct the defence at the hearing, he must have done so feeling that the odds were stacked against his client. Yet Tench had clearly been busy. His first witness was Mrs. Williams, the mother of the accused. She stated that she had had a difficult pregnancy with Henry and that he had always been a strange lad. He had either been very excitable or morose. Gaskin had also found it hard to make friends with other boys. Mrs. Williams felt that her son had been more depressed when he had returned from France and that he had smoked heavily, an act which made him tremble. She also made it clear that Harry was very badly affected by drink and that he was not a regular drinker. Mrs. Williams told of the row in 1917 when her son had threatened to shoot Lizzie if she did not clear off. On the day of the murder, she said that her son had gone to the cinema with Herbert Junemann, her step son. This was confirmed by

Junemann, who made it clear that Gaskin had been in a state of high excitement on the night concerned.

Tench then called Ernest Woodall and Charles Dawson, both of whom had served with Gaskin at Ypres. These two soldiers confirmed that Gaskin had been buried alive following a counter mine explosion and that since then he had been prone to taking unnecessary risks whilst serving at the Front.

The Bench then asked Gaskin to make his plea and the miner from Cannock pleaded "Not Guilty". The prisoner was then committed for trial at Stafford Assizes on the 4th July 1919. He was granted a certificate for defence under the Poor Prisoners' Defence Act.

## Chapter Thirteen

# ON TRIAL FOR HIS LIFE

Gaskin's trial was conducted in the oak panelled court room at Stafford on Friday 4th July 1919. The Judge appointed to hear the case was the Honourable Sir A. Adair Roche. The prosecution case was presented by Mr. C. F. Vachell K. C. assisted by Mr. Grenville Ram. The defence was put by Mr. Graham Milward who was advised by Mr. R. A. Tench who had been Gaskin's solicitor both at the inquest and the committal hearing at Cannock.

Gaskin wore a light coloured suit, with a blue tie and a soft white collar. When the indictment was read out to him, he replied in a firm, clear voice, "Not Guilty".

Vachell smoothly put his case before the jury, emphasising the ferocity of the murder and claiming it was perhaps the most horrible crime that he had ever put before twelve good men and true. He went through the now familiar and sad tale of the Gaskins marriage and subsequent problems due to the infidelity of Mrs. Gaskin, whilst her husband was in prison and in France. Vachell was keen to impress on the jury the fact that Gaskin had been very angry during his leave in 1917 and that he had found his wife's attention in February 1919, both unnecessary and annoying.

The witnesses were then summoned to give their evidence. Once again the case clearly showing Gaskin's guilt was put before a jury, as it had been at the hearing. The same witnesses were called and gave the same evidence. The noose appeared to be tightening around Gaskin's neck.

Milward's defence revolved around a number of issues. The amount that Gaskin had drunk before the murder was important. Milward built up the view that Gaskin was neither a heavy nor a regular drinker. Indeed, this was confirmed not only by Gaskin's mother, but also by Mrs. Talbot, a woman who would hardly have felt a need to do any favours for Henry Thomas Gaskin. John Thomas Garry's evidence was therefore crucial to the defence. The volume of alcohol was confirmed as being considerable by Garry, although his evidence did give a little light relief for the court, when Garry claimed the drinks had not been very strong. This was nipped in the bud by Justice Roche, who rightly felt that a capital trial was not the venue for such levity. Nevertheless, it was now clear to the jury that Gaskin had consumed an unusually large quantity of alcohol over a relatively short period of time.

Milward's next point was the mental state of Gaskin at the time of the murder. He managed to paint a picture of Gaskin being far from normal. Childhood experiences were brought before the jury which strongly indicated that Harry Gaskin was a little below the norm when it came to his mental stability. Perhaps the crucial evidence came from the two soldiers that had served with Gaskin on the Western Front. Both Woodhall and Dawson made it very clear that in their opinion, Gaskin had begun to behave very erratically after he was buried alive in a German counter explosion. The strangeness of Gaskin's manner was also commented upon by a number of the prosecution witnesses during their evidence.

Indeed in his closing speech, Milward claimed that Gaskin had been "abominably used and abominably treated" by his wife. He went on to argue "Insanity moves in waves, and they might have a man, shaky from youth, who might be so wrought, upon the blowing up of a mine in France, and the drink partaken on the day of the deed, that when the moment came, his mind was not right". Milward made the point that the horrific nature of the attack on the day clearly indicated that the prisoner was of unsound mind.

The judge then summed up for the benefit of the jury. Adair Roche made it clear to the members of the jury that Mrs. Gaskin's infidelity did not give Gaskin the right to take private vengeance. The fall from a moral life by the victim was not a crime punishable by law and certainly not a crime punishable by death.

With this advice still firmly ringing in their ears, the jury retired at twenty eight minutes past four. Gaskin would have been taken to the cells immediately below the dock in the Crown Court at Stafford. If Gaskin felt that a long wait would indicate that his counsel had managed to put a measure of doubt in the minds of the jury, then he was to be sorely disappointed. The jury returned at fifty two minutes past four, only a mere twenty four minutes later. As Gaskin mounted the steps back into the dock, he must have known what awaited him. The foreman of the jury announced to the hushed court that they found the prisoner, Henry Thomas Gaskin, guilty of the wilful murder of his wife, Elizabeth Gaskin.

Adair Roche asked Gaskin if he had anything to say before he passed sentence upon him. In a quiet and steady voice, Gaskin replied, "I did not intend to kill her". The judge then went on to express the opinion that the verdict was a right and proper one. He then donned the black cap, as was the tradition, and in a sombre voice informed Gaskin that he would be taken to a place of execution where he would hang by the neck until he was dead. The judge then, again as was traditional, hoped that the Almighty would have mercy upon Gaskin's soul. With those words, Gaskin was taken down from the dock and was then driven back to Winson Green Prison to await his fate.

Milward was not yet finished. He felt that he had good grounds for an appeal. Whether he informed Gaskin of this before he left Stafford, or whether it was shortly after Gaskin's arrival at Winson Green, is not known. The appeal would have to be put forward quickly, and indeed, at the Appeal Court in London, on 21st July 1919, Milward made his appeal on behalf of his client. The appeal went before Mr. Justice Darling and Mr. Justice Sankey. Milward's line of argument was that Gaskin should not have been found guilty because of his insanity at the time of the crime. This part of the appeal was dismissed due to no conclusive evidence being offered at the trial. His second line of appeal was that Mr. Justice Roche had failed to instruct the jury that they could have found Gaskin guilty of manslaughter, due to provocation by his wife. The two Appeal Court judges thought long and hard but could find no evidence of such provocation. As a result the original verdict was a sound one and the appeal was turned down. The date for the execution was set for Friday 8th August 1919.

On the following day in Winson Green Prison, Birmingham, Henry Thomas Gaskin passed his 28th birthday. He did so knowing that his life would be extinguished in precisely eighteen days.

If the judicial process could do no more for Gaskin, it did not mean that nothing more could be done. Presumably initiated by his family, signatures were sought for a memorial to be presented to the Home Secretary. The fact that Gaskin had been found guilty could not be overturned. However, this was not the purpose of the memorial. The aim here was to put pressure on the Home Secretary to commute the death sentence, to one of life imprisonment. There was a considerable groundswell of opinion in the area, that Gaskin had been provoked by his wife's behaviour, and that in view of this, he should not suffer hanging. The response was quite amazing. Over six thousand people were willing to put their name to a plea for clemency. The memorial for Gaskin was sent to the Home Secretary, Edward Shortt. Shortt was unmoved by the plea for mercy. The execution would take place as planned.

The last few days of Gaskin's life no doubt seemed like an eternity. His mind would have been in turmoil, and nothing would have seemed sensible or reasonable to him. During those last few tense, trying, days, he was visited by his mother, step father and some of his relatives. These brief encounters would have been sad, heart rending affairs. Both Gaskin and his visitors would have been choked with raw emotion. Yet even in these last hopeless moments of his life, Gaskin asked his family to thank, on his behalf, all of the people who had supported him, especially those who had organised the memorial to Edward Shortt.

## Chapter Fourteen

# SOME FINAL THOUGHTS

Whichever way one approaches the Gaskin story, one is met by a tragedy. The early years of both the Talbot and Gaskin families were littered with misfortunes of one sort or another. The later years were no less troublesome.

There is evidence that from childhood, Gaskin was a strange boy. Certainly, part of the problem was poor health, and perhaps, an over protective mother. However, this does not explain the attempt to throttle himself around the age of seven. This strongly suggests a measure of instability and latent temper.

The problem also does not help to understand why the young Gaskin found school not to his liking. Truancy, in his case, led to an incident which no doubt left him deeply disturbed; the sexual assault on his sister.

Gaskin's relationship with his father is of interest. There is little evidence of a strong father and son bond. Henry Gaskin senior seems to have found his son's errant behaviour totally bewildering. By 1906, when Harry Gaskin was sent to Saltley, it is fairly clear that Gaskin senior had all but washed his hands of any responsibility for his son's actions. The fact that Gaskin senior failed to attend the first hearing and refused to pay the fine is supportive of this conclusion.

Indeed, even when Harry Gaskin left the Reformatory and joined the army, the subsequent inglorious failure after less than two months would have further damaged the relationship between the two men.

The period from 1910 and 1912 seems to have been a quiet one in Harry Gaskin's life. He had returned to his parents' home, probably at the behest of his mother. His parents were no doubt hopeful that Harry had turned a corner in his life. By 1912, Harry was now approaching 20, was in a steady, if dangerous job down the pit, and had taken some responsibility, in terms of being a scout leader and in being a member of local bands.

Unfortunately, Harry Gaskin was a complicated and seemingly frustrated young man. The series of highway robberies in 1912 suggest a man who lived in a fantasy world. The crimes themselves were serious and shocking, both for the victims and the community as a whole. Yet they display an insight into the world of Harry Gaskin. On the morning of the third robbery, Gaskin was cleaning the floor in the kitchen and scullery at St. John's Road. His mother and father had gone to the hospital. Harry was a dutiful son when he wished to be. His actions on that day are also unpredictable. After robbing Mary Jelliman of one shilling, odd in itself as she had four shillings, he then agreed to walk with her past two men whom she was nervous about passing. These are hardly the actions of a vicious criminal.

Gaskin's marriage to Elizabeth Talbot in 1913 was a crucial act in the tragedy. That Elizabeth was pregnant obviously hastened the proceedings. However, it appears as if Elizabeth Talbot lied to Harry Gaskin in terms of the paternity of her unborn child. It says a lot about Gaskin in that he was willing to accept his responsibilities. His marriage may also have triggered the spree of burglaries that saw Harry Gaskin imprisoned for three years in 1914.

Incarceration followed by army service had an enormous impact upon Gaskin. Whether he was aware of his wife's drift into prostitution is not clear. It is possible that his mother had kept him up to date on the sordid tale. This could explain why Gaskin chose not to return to his wife on his release from prison in 1916, instead deciding to go straight into the army.

The experiences of Harry Gaskin in the Great War help one to understand the events of February 19th, 1919. His leave in 1917 left him in no doubt about his wife's lack of fidelity. It also showed that the war had had an impact on the mental state of Harry Gaskin. For the first time, Gaskin displayed an extreme rage, threatening to shoot his wife. The leave also showed the caring, almost romantic, side of his nature. His second leave only confirmed that his marriage was in shreds; his wife choosing to ply her trade in London. Gaskin's mother showed that she was now really concerned about the unpredictable nature of her son, deciding not to pass on a letter from Lizzie Gaskin.

Gaskin's return to Cannock in 1919 had an immense impact upon a war weary, confused man. The impact of being buried alive, whilst serving in the Royal Engineers, had left Gaskin in an unbalanced mental state. This was exacerbated with the news that his wife had given birth to another child. Gaskin was annoyed by his wife's desire to begin the relationship again. He felt that this was not what he wanted; Gaskin preferred a divorce.

Whether Harry Gaskin set out with the intention of murdering his wife on February 19th, 1919, is by no means certain. A miner carrying a lamp hook and knife in his pocket was commonplace. Gaskin knew that he faced a difficult time coming to terms with his wife's actions, but there is nothing to suggest intent. He was extremely drunk, angry, confused and disturbed. Whatever it was that tipped him over the edge on that day will never be known. The suggestion that it was the discovery that he was not the father of his son, Arthur can only be, at best, conjecture.

Whether Gaskin did intend to kill his wife was a moot point once the jury at his trial read his confession. The act of brutal and depraved butchery of his wife was enough to gain a guilty verdict in only 24 minutes.

Gaskin's subsequent failed appeal against his sentence, and his last few days before his execution, give a glimpse of a man who had come to terms with his fate. He accepted that nothing more could be done for him. The humanity of Gaskin comes through with his request that people, who had tried to reduce his sentence to one of imprisonment, should be thanked. That he walked to his death with firm footsteps is a measure of the courage of Harry Gaskin.

Yet, Gaskin's actions had left two families in tatters. The Talbot family had, over a matter of seven years, lost a daughter, a son and two daughters in law. Harriett Williams had lost a daughter, a husband and now her beloved son, Harry. She may have taken a macabre pride in the fact that the wood where the murder took place became known colloquially as "Gaskin's Wood". One thing is certain, in the following years, and Harriett Williams lived until the age of 73, there would not have been a day when she did not think about her son.